RAISING

Waldorf

**The Building
of the
Waldorf School
on the
Roaring Fork**

ISBN-13: 978-0-9789735-0-6
ISBN-10: 0-9789735-0-x

Printed in the United States of America.

Publishers: Barbi and Doug Sheffer
Writer: Patricia L. Fox
Editor: Stewart Oksenhorn
Coordinator: Eleanor Jacobs
Photography: Stevan Maxwell
Design: Lynn Crawford

Managing Editor: J. Sue Robertson
Waldorf Editorial Consultant: Eugene Schwartz
Printer: Pyramid Printing, Grand Junction, Colorado

The narrative in this book is a story told by many
but no one embodied the soul of the school quite
like Steven Moore. It is to his memory
that this book is dedicated.

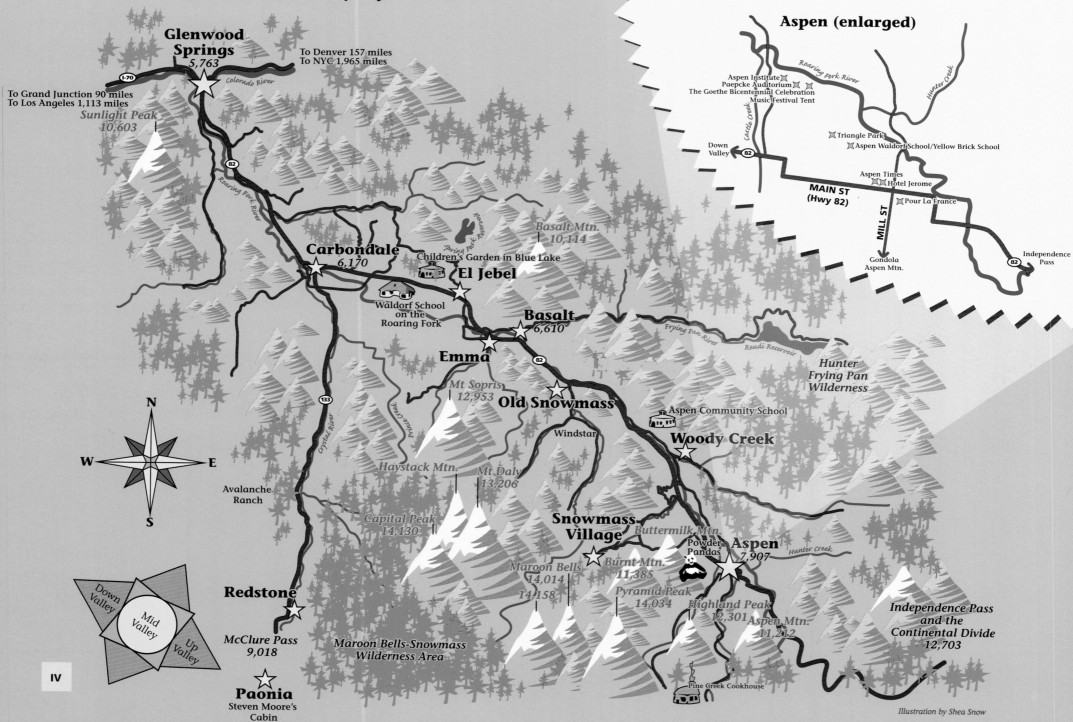

The Roaring Fork Valley of Colorado

Glenwood Springs 5,763

To Denver 157 miles
To NYC 1,965 miles

To Grand Junction 90 miles
To Los Angeles 1,113 miles

Sunlight Peak 10,603

Colorado River

Roaring Fork River

I-70

82

Carbondale 6,170

Spring Park Reservoir

Children's Garden in Blue Lake

Basalt Mtn. 10,114

El Jebel

Waldorf School on the Roaring Fork

Basalt 6,610

Frying Pan River

Reudi Reservoir

Emma

Mt Sopris 12,953

Old Snowmass

Windstar

Hunter Frying Pan Wilderness

Aspen Community School

Woody Creek

133

Crystal River

Prince Creek

Haystack Mtn.

Mt Daly 13,206

Avalanche Ranch

Capital Peak 14,130

Snowmass Village

Buttermilk Mtn.

Powder Pandas

Aspen 7,907

Hunter Creek

N
W E
S

Down Valley
Mid Valley
Up Valley

Redstone

Maroon Bells 14,014 14,158

Burnt Mtn. 11,385

Pyramid Peak 14,034

Highland Peak 12,301

Aspen Mtn. 11,212

Independence Pass and the Continental Divide 12,703

McClure Pass 9,018

Maroon Bells-Snowmass Wilderness Area

IV

Paonia
Steven Moore's Cabin

Pine Creek Cookhouse

Illustration by Shea Snow

Aspen (enlarged)

Roaring Fork River

Hunter Creek

Aspen Institute
Paepcke Auditorium
The Goethe Bicentennial Celebration
Music Festival Tent

Castle Creek

Triangle Park

Aspen Waldorf School/Yellow Brick School

Down Valley

82

Aspen Times
Hotel Jerome

MAIN ST (Hwy 82)

MILL ST

Pour La France

Independence Pass

Gondola Aspen Mtn.

82

v

Barbi and Doug Sheffer

Introduction

When I first approached Patty Fox, a founder of the Aspen Waldorf School, to write a history of the school, we asked, "Who would read it?" After all, the school was a small initiative by a small group of parents in a small town in remote western Colorado. But the biography of this school is the biography of human endeavor. Like the biography of a single human being, it is a story, the sum total of all of the stories of those involved. It is the birth of a school, which involves Aspen, Colorado, mothers, fathers, children, great ideas, risk-taking, heart-felt feelings, a business and something mysterious besides.

First, there was the town of Aspen itself. Set in the upper reaches of the Roaring Fork River watershed, Aspen has always been a place of intensities and extremes. In the high elevations of the Roaring Fork Valley (one and one-half to nearly three miles above sea level), the thinner air creates less of a barrier to the forces of Nature.

The intense sunlight and surrounding 14,000-foot peaks create weather: resounding thunderstorms in the summer and abundant snows in the winter. Thinner air equates to less atmospheric pressure, giving rise to a sense of freedom of spirit, of levity, and closeness to the heavens. One feels elevated both literally and spiritually. To gaze at the stars from the perspective of the highest Waldorf school in North America evokes feelings of hope, endless possibilities and unlimited potential.

These elements are certainly what drew the Ute Native Americans, the silver miners, the skiing pioneers, and eventually the Chicago intellectuals/entrepreneurs, Elizabeth and Walter Paepcke, to Aspen. It was they who staged the Goethe Bicentennial in 1949, resulting in Dr. Albert Schweitzer's only journey from Africa to America. Schweitzer addressed the crowd of two thousand with a message of transcending one's own existence in service of humanity and the greater good.

Schweitzer's message was, in turn, inspired by the thoughts and deeds of Johann Wolfgang von Goethe, writer, poet, philosopher and scientist, whose 200th birthday was the occasion for the gathering in Aspen.

Several decades before this seed was planted in Aspen, Goethe's ideas had profoundly influenced the European scientist and philosopher Rudolf Steiner. Steiner developed a pedagogical system known as "Waldorf education" that was based on Goethean principles. Years later, when a group of parents were gathered together, teetering on the brink of starting the Aspen Waldorf School, Goethe's message – powerfully expressed by both Schweitzer and Steiner – came full circle. In effect, Goethe had returned to Aspen, this time in the form of an educational philosophy.

Of course, we are all a bit idealistic when it comes to starting new enterprises; the same innocence applies to our relationships, marriages, and parenting. Luckily we had the skills of an experienced teacher to help guide us. Patty Fox brought the framework of Waldorf Education to our group. She showed us that Steiner suggested the life of an initiative such as ours could be understood as having stages of development similar to that of an individual human being. By anthropomorphizing human activities, one can observe cycles of the school, just as in a child, in seven-year groups. Ideally, we could have used these observations to head-off minor issues and problems before they became major influences in the life of the school, but we were going through our own life cycles, and so our success, at times, was limited by some missed cues and opportunities.

This past fall, our school entered the third cycle of youth. In our first seven-year cycle, we were like young children, too busy "doing" to stop and assess. During the middle elementary years, when true emotions are engaged, thoughtful contemplation wasn't even considered an option. Now that we are fifteen years old, we can begin to look back, learn from our past and enter the mid-adolescent stage of thinking.

We want to thank you in advance for reading this book, the purchase price of which goes towards financially supporting the school. Perhaps in reliving our first two cycles of life, you will share with us our ecstatic joy of birth, the love and sense of community with which we surrounded the children, our disappointment and sorrows, our tremendous sense of accomplishment in the moving and building of a campus, and finally a realistic acceptance of an unfolding life known as the Waldorf School on the Roaring Fork (WSRF).

As you page through the book, please note that in its earlier years, the school is referred to as the Aspen Waldorf School (AWS). It was not until the move to Carbondale that the school was given its present name. This book is an effort to reflect the many human encounters, meetings and decisions that characterize an entity as alive and changing as the Waldorf School on the Roaring Fork. The present strength and vitality of the school is the result of efforts made by teachers, staff and parents since the school's birth, and we continue to build on that foundation. Even in the two years it has taken to bring this book to press a number of changes and improvements have taken place in such areas as parent education, faculty retention, remedial education and school governance. You will find a full description of our progress in the Afterword.

We hope that our story will further your story as you build your school, your business, your non-profit organization or combine your talents with others for the greater good in service of humankind.

Doug Sheffer
Publisher

Aspen, Colorado
August 23, 2006

Chapter 1

Gestation

Our gestation was brief, perhaps too brief to bring forth the perfect body for a school that needed so many helping hands and feet, fingers and toes. But fools rush in and we who founded the school wanted to give our own and many other school-age children the best. For us, it could only be a Waldorf education. We cannot say in what spiritual realm the marriage that brought us all together took place, but the first flutter of the heartbeat to be heard in the wider community was a workshop organized by Karinjo DeVore. In July of 1990, Merlyn and René Querido, respectively teacher and director at Rudolf Steiner College (RSC) in Sacramento, were in Aspen for the Aspen Music Festival and Karinjo asked if they would conduct a workshop.

Patty Fox, another local mother interested in Waldorf, was disappointed to read that the workshop had taken place while she had been backpacking, but her sister-in-law, Jennifer Fox, a founder of the City of the Lakes Waldorf School in Minneapolis, was coming to visit. She knew the Queridos and arranged for a lunch meeting. Patty, Jennifer, Merlyn and René sat on the Pour la France! patio chatting amiably about Waldorf education when René said pointedly to Patty, "You could start a school here! This is the home of the Goethe Bicentennial. A Waldorf school would thrive." It was the call of destiny.

Patty met Karinjo, who introduced her to Betsy Engelman, another Waldorf enthusiast. The three women were galvanized and in August, Patty enrolled in an introductory course at RSC. She returned inspired to share Waldorf ideas at the local college that fall and when Ideas from the Waldorf Kindergarten ended, an ad hoc committee, Friends of Waldorf in Aspen, was formed. It was as if the Angel of the Aspen Waldorf School began whispering in the Friends' ears but the thought of starting a private school was daunting and elitist. A new elementary school was being built. Couldn't we sponsor a Waldorf track within it which parents could choose? The first public Waldorf school was opening in Milwaukee. It would be our model.

Led by Patty and Jim Fox, Betsy and Bill Engelman, Barbi and Doug Sheffer, and Karinjo DeVore, the Friends held public lectures (with lovely refreshments and careful décor) to educate public school teachers, school board members and especially the general public about Waldorf education. Joan Condon, Cheryl Mulholland and Bill Fordham, teachers from the Denver Waldorf School, and Betty Staley and René Querido from RSC spoke to audiences that sometimes numbered over a hundred.

In January of 1991, the Friends formally proposed a public-private partnership to the Aspen School District. The new Aspen Elementary School would provide the space and we would provide the salary and supplies for a trial Waldorf first grade. With hand-painted personal invitations, we continued to encourage the public school teachers to attend workshops and dinners but only two teachers, Peter Westcott and Anita Strickbine, ever did. After four months and more private and public meetings, the school board refused our request saying sufficient study had not been done. We vowed to try again – and did, with an unsuccessful charter school proposal three years later.

Late that fall, Patty attended a conference at the Shining Mountain Waldorf School in Boulder where three leaders of the movement, René Querido, Werner Glas and Eugene Schwartz, lectured. When Eugene agreed to speak in Aspen, too, (He loved to ski!) another lasting relationship began. Eugene was a scholarly and charismatic spokesman with long experience as a Waldorf class teacher and mentor. His lecture in March was our first successful fundraising effort.

At Pine Creek Cookhouse, Karinjo, CP Kanipe and Patty tried to entice Carol Nimick (second from left) to become their Waldorf teacher in the public school in 1990.

Aspen parents pushing for alternative education

BY DONNA DANIELS

A group of Aspen parents is pushing the local school district to offer an alternative to public school education, a program they hope will be in place this fall, and eventually spread downvalley.

With schools under fire for providing less than acceptable education these days, and test scores under par, parents are becoming more involved in school curriculum, said spokeswoman Patty Fox. The Aspen-based grass-roots

However, Fox said both the Aspen school board and the superintendent of schools, Tom Farrell, have expressed support.

The idea to bring the Waldorf method to Aspen started about two years ago, Fox said. There are now 140 people interested in seeing it start up, parents who want

the program has been a perception that kids coming out of it are not prepared to face mainstream education. But Fox said the Waldorf students she's met have not had problems fitting in.

She does admit, however, that a real problem could exist in finding a Waldorf-trained teacher.

"Committing to a particular philosophy may not be appropriate. We want to be able to adjust our teaching strategy to meet a student's needs."

Howard Jay
Carbondale Elementary Principal

Thursday, January 31, 1991   Times Daily 7

Education innovators want local schools to treat a kid like a kid

By TERRI BARTELSTEIN
Times Daily Staff Writer

A group of local parents would like the already-progressive Aspen school system to become even more innovative by adding an alternative grade school class for "Waldorf-inspired" education.

Waldorf education, which dates back to turn of the century Europe, is a method and philosophy that integrates academic subject matter with the emotional and intellectual development of the child.

"It's a different view of the child – a child is not

"What we're proposing is a partnership between the private sector and the public school system."

education innovator

24-C • The Aspen Times June 13, 1991

Friends of Waldorf plan kids' summer camp with Windstar

by Brighid Kelly
Windstar will host a camp for youngsters this summer

ence. The youngsters will have one activity with the Waldorf

...ldorf kindergarten ...ay and week has a ...ring the summer ...ys include baking; ...feature watercolor ...Thursdays, a craft. ...egin with free play ...activity followed ...rcle games, stories ...outdoor free play, ...oodbye verse, and

...most of the child- ...but they can nap ...indstar with the ...hey're tired. ...en will also sing ...s, play outdoors ...vities. Ordinarily ...ours of the first ...ning would be ...the main lesson,

noon hike with kindergartners.

In addition to day classes, there will be a series of evening workshops and lectures by the teachers which will be open to all parents valleywide.

Thursday evening, July 25 will be "Arts in the Waldorf Kindergarten-First Grade." Wednesday evening, July 31 will be "Developing the Environment for Creative Play at Home and School," and Tuesday, Aug 6 will be "Rhythm in the Life of the Young Child." Time, locations and specific activities will be announced later.

The Waldorf initiative in Aspen has gained momentum during its two years of existence. During the summer, several additional workshops are planned and the group expects to open a first- and second-grade class, as well as

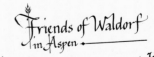

Friends of Waldorf in Aspen

Newsletter #3   July, 1991

The Aspen Waldorf School--A Dream Come True!

At the organizational Board Meeting July ...elve parents and community members voted ...imously to open The Aspen Waldorf School ...eptember, 1991. The decision was thoughtful ...d obvious--when we considered all of the ...wing:

Teachers. At present, we have secured ...services of our two hoped-for teachers, Patty ...yle, for first/second grade, and Stephanie ...vins for the mixed-age kindergarten (3 to 6 year ...ds).

Location. We have a plethora of ...sible locations on which we will be making a ...decision within the month. If none of the

We also have some guarantor money for the first year and are looking for more. It's very do-able.

Calendar. During August, we will have a parents' meeting to discuss the length of the school day for all children and the calendar for the year.

So! What could we have decided but YES! YES! YES!

Committee Reports

Several committees were organized at the July 1 Board Meeting. Their preliminary reports follow:

Executive Committee. The Executive ...will be made up of the officers of the

By this time, we had put enormous effort into public awareness and had planned a summer camp to showcase the benefits of Waldorf education. Our camp, Waldorf at Windstar, was also the best deal to be had in the Roaring Fork Valley! For $100, parents could send their preschoolers, kindergarteners and first graders to an all-day camp at Windstar for three weeks, transportation from Aspen included, thanks to Doug Sheffer. Taught by Denver Waldorf teachers, Dana Fordham and Lin Welsh in the kindergarten and Patty Doyle, freshly plucked from RSC, in the first grade, the camp was wildly successful by every measure. In the midst of it, on July 1, 1991, the Friends met on the top floor of the Sardy House, which housed Patty Fox's office as executive director of the Aspen Writers' Foundation. There, buoyed by full enrollment in the camp and bonded by a year of adventure and adversity, twelve Friends voted unanimously to open the Aspen Waldorf School in September.

Our confidence was bolstered by the fact that we thought we had secured the services of two trained teachers. Though inexperienced, Patty Doyle was perfect for the first grade. She had grown up in Aspen, graduated from the University of Colorado, and traveled in Europe, where she had met Waldorf education. She'd returned to the two-year teacher training at RSC and when ready to graduate, René Querido had told her she really had no choice but to help found a new Waldorf school in Aspen. At twenty-five, Patty little suspected what this meant and though full of enthusiasm, she considered offers from several established European schools before she agreed to join us.

Stephanie Blevins, also a trained class teacher, had moved to the valley with her husband, Bruce, a biodynamic gardener. She had assisted Dana and had agreed to be our kindergarten teacher but on the last day of the camp, she delivered a heavy blow. Uncertain of our enrollment, she had decided to accept a teaching position with the new public Waldorf school in

Milwaukee. We couldn't blame her for having doubts, but who could teach our kindergarten? There was one teacher among us and Dana pointed to Patty Fox, who had ten years of teaching experience and a master's degree in education. With Dana's promise to mentor, Patty took up the work of the kindergarten. CP (Patricia) Kanipe agreed to assist her – but only until her massage business picked up at Thanksgiving.

Upper: Maureen Fox (front), Marina Kanipe and Melinda Engelman in Bill Fordham's Windstar classroom

Lower: Dana Fordham's Waldorf-at-Windstar kindergarten

The search for a space for a kindergarten and a combined first/second grade began simultaneously with an application for 501(c) 3 non-profit status, formation of a board of trustees, writing articles of incorporation and by-laws, securing liability insurance, and being licensed by the state as a preschool/kindergarten. Patty's computer on the top floor was humming! While the Aspen School Board would not agree to our track proposal, they did agree to lease space to us in the soon-to-be-vacated Yellow Brick School. We would occupy the building with independent infant and child care operations.

However, the Aspen Elementary School would not vacate their old building until November and only after desperate searching and through grace did we find Mimi Schlumberger, director of the children's ski school at Buttermilk Mountain, and the Aspen Skiing Company willing to rent space to us in the interim. Powder Pandas was nestled in golden aspen trees, a magical space in which to give birth. On September 9th, 1991, the bulging womb opened to reveal the Aspen Waldorf School: nine first graders, ten kindergarteners and three teachers named Patty.

© Nicholas DeVore III

© Nicholas DeVore III

Upper and lower:
Bill Fordham's Windstar
classroom, 1992

Upper: Karinjo DeVore
Lower: Barbi and Doug Sheffer drive Dana and the children to camp

Karinjo DeVore

She brought a seed from South Africa to plant in Aspen.

"Waldorf brings a different understanding of how the world works."

Much of what I love about Waldorf education is its celebration of the enchanting mysteries of life. In that spirit I suggest that a tiny seed for the Aspen Waldorf School was gathered in the Maluti Mountains of Africa.

When my mother returned to South Africa, the land of her childhood, I remained in Aspen in protest of the wrongs of apartheid. I was "adopted" by Aspen ski pioneer, Jony Poschman Larrowe, who captivated me with stories of her childhood at a Steiner School in Bavarian Germany during Hitler's rise. When the S.S. soldiers would approach the mountain-top school, which was disguised as a retreat for sickly children, the students would cease their studies and cover themselves in blankets on cots.

After completing a degree in fine arts and art history, I set out on adventures elsewhere in the world. I herded goats in the South of France, taught skiing in the Alps, traveled across Afghanistan on camel, trekked past the peaks of K-2 headed for the mysteries of Hunza before being captured by Chinese soldiers. With this diverse experience, I was offered a position in the Kingdom of Lesotho, an independent enclave surrounded by South Africa. I would work with a British foundation to support traditional artists.

The British production of *Jesus Christ Superstar* came to Lesotho in 1970 with a support cast from Johannesburg. When I learned they had all graduated from the Johannesburg Waldorf School, I heard the echo of Jony's stories. I was intrigued by their discussions of anthroposophy, the temperaments, color and sound. They shared their network of Waldorf friends and wherever I traveled in South Africa, I met fascinating, like-minded people. I decided that if ever I had children, they would have a Waldorf education.

After ten years in Africa, I returned to Aspen, where I married Nicholas. While pregnant with our son Niki, I met Pam Doble and Betsy Engelman and we later shared an aesthetic that preferred healthy surroundings with organic foods, natural fibers and diapers, wooden toys and nursing. I dreamed of an educational environment where Niki would be nourished and thrive and together we began our explorations into alternative education, including Waldorf.

At a party I talked to an engaging woman named Cheryl Mulholland, who introduced herself as a Waldorf teacher in Hawaii. Several weeks later she wrote to tell me that René Querido, director of Rudolf Steiner College, would be coming to the Aspen Music Festival and would be pleased to conduct a workshop. The fifty-plus participants were all delighted with the lectures, stories, eurythmy and math games, and Merlyn and René touched everyone present. They encouraged us to continue our studies and promised help in the establishment of a future school.

That fall Patty Fox taught her class at Colorado Mountain College and we began trying to persuade the public school to initiate a Waldorf track. The superintendent, Dr. Frank Betts, was quite enthusiastic, as was Betsy Hill, the principal of the middle school. We thought the public schools had a chance to be truly innovative and that they were short-sighted not to see the value of this group of parents who were willing to raise the salary and expenses for Waldorf classes and teachers and expand the options for education. After our proposal was rejected and we had decided to found a private school, we met with the school board to request space for our classrooms in the Yellow Brick School, which the Aspen Elementary School was about to vacate. Unexpectedly, the teachers gathered in such strong opposition that we were stunned. The school board later apologized and agreed to lease space to us.

I was one of the twelve who on July 1, 1991, voted to start the school. I was so hopeful. We began recruiting – and signed up one girl after another, but not one other boy. I was heartbroken, but knew I could not expect my active, athletic Niki to be happy in a class of girls, and as a board member, I wanted the first years of our school to flow as smoothly as possible. My daughter Katrina attended the Waldorf pre-school, danced in the Maypole and together we relished the kindergarten experience. When she transferred to Aspen Country Day School to follow her brother, she insisted on having Patty Fox come to her class for her special Waldorf birthday celebration.

Beyond my family, though, Waldorf brings a different understanding of how the world works: that a seed gathered in Africa could be planted here in Aspen. It's wonderful to have Waldorf in the Roaring Fork Valley and I know that its presence has an invaluable and mysterious effect. Perhaps my grandchildren will go to a Waldorf school.

Merlyn Querido

Merlyn and René Querido, leaders of Waldorf education worldwide, had confidence in our dream to start a new school and this gave us courage.

My sister had a house in Aspen in the 50's and so I came here often as a young woman. René and I had found a small hotel with a kitchen that we could afford on our teacher's salary at the Shining Mountain Waldorf School in Boulder. We stayed for two weeks in the summers, attending master classes and concerts at the Music Festival. I remember rainstorms during concerts in the early days when water would collect on the tent and come swishing down in the middle of someone's singing. It was a wonderful place to be in the summer and we came back even when René became Director of Rudolf Steiner College in Sacramento.

Karinjo DeVore asked us to give a workshop on Waldorf education at Star Mesa in the summer of 1990 and later we spoke to a gathering in June Kirkwood's living room. We were very fond of both women but when we met Patty Fox, we really thought a school might be started in Aspen. Patty and her sister-in-law, Jennifer, who knew René from the City of the Lakes Waldorf School in Minneapolis, invited us for lunch at Pour la France! I can still remember where we sat – and how excited René was at the possibility of a school here, home of the Goethe Bicentennial.

René had a wonderful gift. He was never critical and had great confidence in people and their dreams. This gave them courage and so he started many schools. When he returned to his young schools to lecture, the teachers and parents would say his enthusiasm kept them going for a whole year.

René built things that prospered and I know many devoted anthroposophists who tried to do this but couldn't. It was an intangible quality, but very real.

We often stayed with Barbi and Doug Sheffer when we came to Aspen, which we tried to do every year although René had his first kidney operation in 1991 and spent a year recovering. In 1994, when some people wanted to become a charter school, René was there to say, "Go ahead with your plans. This may work out for you but the Aspen Waldorf School will remain independent." The school needed his confidence to survive in those early years.

"René built things that prospered."

Lisa Fortier and Kathryn King host a dinner/lecture with René

Patty Fox

Patty gathered the critical mass of founders and eight years later graduated the pioneer class.

My journey to Waldorf education began when my first child, Maureen, came back to me four days after her caesarean birth, a flight for life and intensive care in Denver. When I held her then, I was deeply, irrevocably aware that I was not holding the product of a biological process. She was an angelic, spiritual being who came to me just as Wordsworth had said, "trailing clouds of glory." I wept during those precious newborn weeks first because I had been granted this knowledge, as I think all mothers are, and second, because for the ten years I'd taught in public schools, I'd not recognized the spiritual being in hundreds of other children. My quest for an education that recognized the individuality, the "I," had begun.

That my quest should lead me to Waldorf was, I suppose, destined. My first husband grew up in Germany and his extended family had served on the board of trustees of the original Waldorf school in Stuttgart. Later, when I lived with his sister in Sacramento, I drove past Rudolf Steiner College every day on my way to teach my public school class. I always felt a pull, but I never pulled in. When my current sister-in-law, Jennifer, found a Waldorf preschool for her daughter in Minneapolis and excitedly called me about it, the tug grew stronger.

She enrolled her daughter and began to immerse herself in Waldorf education. When I called her for mothering advice, her words were filled with wisdom and practicality that resonated with truth. I had to learn more.

My learning, at first, was through the Hearthsong catalogue, a Waldorf-inspired catalogue of children's toys. This was a materialistic introduction to a non-materialistic education but I watched how Maureen, and later Matthew, played with silk scarves and wooden cars and their play had a more wholesome quality than play with plastic toys. In the summer of 1990, I met Karinjo De-Vore and Betsy Engelman, mothers who shared my enthusiasm. When I received a mailing describing two week-long classes for parents at RSC I felt I simply had to attend, despite the fact that I had never left my children, now six and almost four, even overnight.

Above: Patty's kindergarten celebrates Katrina DeVore's birthday, 1992

Right: Dress-up in the kindergarten

My husband Jim stepped up to mother and I flew to Sacramento. When I walked into the Red Rose Kindergarten at the Sacramento Waldorf School, I instantly felt connected. In fact, I'm still close to some of those women, six of whom started new Waldorf schools!

Janet Kellman and Joan Almon, aka Snow White and Rose Red, two of the most respected teachers in Waldorf early childhood education, taught us child development and deep play, music and art, rhythm, ritual and repetition. The second week Brigitta Goldman, another gifted teacher from Austria, taught us to dye silks, make exquisite marionettes and carefully stitch felt table puppets to use in fairy tale plays. I returned inspired to share my new knowledge of children, childhood and family life with anyone who would listen.

As I had taught writing classes at the Aspen campus of Colorado Mountain College, I was permitted to teach Ideas from the Waldorf kindergarten too. The catalogue for fall had already been published and I couldn't wait until spring, so I filled my class by posting flyers in the library and handing them to mothers in the grocery store. With Betsy Engelman's artistic help and joyful hours of preparation, I tried to faithfully reproduce my Sacramento experience for the twenty-eight parents, grandparents and teachers who enrolled. My professors at RSC whom I contacted for advice were, I think, stunned by my audacity – to teach a course in Waldorf education after ten days of exposure! – but they encouraged me and hoped that Waldorf would be decently represented. I guess it was, because when the semester ended, Friends of Waldorf in Aspen, a band of Waldorf converts, had been born.

Our year-long attempt to become part of the public schools failed but we persevered. I spent long hours in the tiny garret of the Aspen Writers' Foundation writing the legal documents we needed to open the Aspen Waldorf School. When I answered the call to step into the kindergarten I thought I could keep my part-time job as executive director, teach kindergarten and continue as president of the new board of trustees. I was leaning heavily on my sister-in-law, Jennifer Fox, who had recently helped to found the City of the Lakes Waldorf School in Minneapolis, but I was completely overwhelmed.

Despite setbacks and meltdowns, we opened. CP and I, with small knowledge but endless good intentions and the gifted mentoring of Dana Fordham, grew our little kindergarten from nine to twenty the first two years and deepened our relationship from casual friends to soul sisters. When Patty Doyle left for New Zealand after our second year, I began the journey of the Waldorf class teacher who ideally takes his or her class from first through eighth grade, a journey of crushing demands and staggering joys. As I had scarcely begun my kindergarten training when the move was decided, I began teaching third grade with only a superficial grasp of the curriculum – as garnered from Eugene Schwartz's lectures to our parents! I invited Marianne Grey to come from RSC to mentor me for two weeks but my long experience as a public school teacher made it difficult, at first, to assimilate Waldorf methods.

RSTUVWXYZ

But students, parents, teachers – we were all pioneers! I continued as president of the board of trustees for three more years, planning festivals and public lectures to publicize our existence. I was as demanding of my students as I was of the parents, feeling they, too, must demonstrate to the community the superiority of a Waldorf education. They never failed me. Main lesson books were beautifully executed. Every play, concert and service deed was stellar. One fifth grade exploit will illustrate: As a fund-raiser, we decided to offer a three course Middle Eastern dinner for sixty people to complement the third grade performance of *Joseph and his Coat of Many Colors*. The class slaved for days with Betsy, Valerie Lee and me to produce an elegant affair. In addition to cooking everything from scratch, we planned and made centerpieces for the rented white linen tables, learned to serve and remove each course, played a recorder concert during dessert and then cleaned up until after midnight! We netted $25.00. We were mad – but we were happy!

I continued my summer teacher training at RSC but frustratingly, my course always covered material for the grade I had just finished teaching. Fortunately, I had teachers there who became friends and mentors, and others – Carol Nimick, Ina Jaenig, Joan Condon, Vicki Carr and Thesa Kallinicos – were also endlessly supportive. The combined class grew from seven to twenty-one with graduations each year from 1996 to 1999! I'm proud of the mark my students made in their high schools as outstanding students, artists, athletes and class officers. Now in college they are successful and innovative, pursuing educations that include selfless service, world culture and politics, and the arts. Although my story ended dissonantly due to the departure of my son's well-loved teacher, I will be forever grateful for the journey traveled with my students and my founding friends near and far.

11

© Nicholas DeVore III

"It was a gift to know the children through their hands."

Betsy Engelman

From the first, Betsy made every event, every project, and every group decision a work of art.

I became acutely aware of what a different education Waldorf was in 1990, the year my daughter, Melinda, entered the public kindergarten. I felt that the school was aesthetically blind and videos served as babysitters. It was disappointing to see how my child's day was filled when I wanted her to be using her imagination and imitating worthy teachers. Patty Fox and I had shared our interest in Waldorf and after she attended a class at Rudolf Steiner College, we would "sneak" into our daughters' kindergarten to do beautiful class projects, painting and sewing felt gnomes. For the holidays we made wooden deer and had to pretend we weren't allowing the children to use the handsaw and drill, but when no one was looking, we taught them to use tools. A knot was tied between us. I backed Patty's ideas, helped her to teach the CMC class, to petition the public schools for a Waldorf track, to organize Friends of Waldorf in Aspen and later, Waldorf at Windstar.

When we opened the school, I was the handwork teacher, on the board of trustees and totally involved in the festivals. It was a joy to see children having fun in such a healthy way and I loved working with the parents on crafts for our monthly festivals. For years I did all of the artwork and calligraphy for our flyers and newsletters. We wanted everything to be beautiful and I think it was. It was beautiful, too, the way we worked together so closely.

The years that I taught at the Waldorf School were the most creative years of my life. Every class wove together a craft that had meaning. We created puppets, scripts and sets to expand main lessons. We felted wool slippers to send to the children at the Tashi Waldorf School which became our sister school in Tibet. It's fun to remember all we learned about children, about how to run an organization, about teaching and, for me, handwork. My son, Glenn, is teaching his Aspen High School tennis team

to knit and when I heard the coach say, "Do you think we could put the knitting down now and go out and play tennis?" I knew a seed had been sown that will bear fruit for many years – in many unexpected places! Artistic work and work with our hands provides us with an incomparable feeling of creative satisfaction.

I have been involved with handwork on a daily basis all my life as my mother was a master of the fiber arts: stitchery, knitting, crochet, crewel and clothing design. As a young adult, the handwork teacher at the Waldorf School in Sebastapol, California was my neighbor and I helped her when she came home with baskets of the children's knitting projects to fix. I was fascinated that first graders were knitting gnomes.

The circle of first grade knitters, 1994

Margareta teaches a handwork class to parents

In the classroom, every lesson was a challenge that required skills I never thought I had, skills and a lot of patience. When I started my teaching at Powder Pandas, I had to drop preconceived ideas. My mom had been such a stickler when she taught me, I thought I could teach a class the same way. I couldn't. When I helped one student, the next would knit her flute case wider and wider rather than longer and longer. But I went to conferences and learned from other handwork teachers. Margareta Eichenholtz, a master teacher, came from Sweden and stayed with me for several weeks. She became a special friend and mentor. When I visited other schools, I realized that their handwork was not any more beautiful than ours; in fact, often it wasn't as beautiful. I slowly gained confidence in my teaching.

I loved to see the children's excitement as they learned a new handwork skill. Understanding the correlation between arts and crafts learned at an early age and the academics that follow reinforced my own intuition about how children learn. The subtleties of color and natural fibers, of taking care in everything we do, of being environmentally conscious and not wasteful were lessons embedded in every class. And I got to do the fun stuff with them! They always looked forward to my class and I've never had a better feeling than sitting in a circle of happy knitters. It was a gift to know the children through their hands, helping them make something beautiful to share with others.

Another gift of my teaching years was that I had a chance to share something intimate and important with my mom at the end of her life. We would work out projects together or I'd send something to her to fix or finish. She sewed the crewel pencil cases the sixth graders made and they're still in great shape!

Everything was woven together in Waldorf. Not only memories of my mom and my daughter, but the ribbon tail of the bluebird that we sewed at Valentine's became the Maypole streamers, then the tail of the kites at Michaelmas. Traditions handed from mother to child live on in Waldorf traditions. All of Melinda's friends have a stuffed animal or flute case that they made. And every Waldorf student she meets will have them too, all different but shared around the world, weaving us together in a special way.

14

Barbi Sheffer

Barbi and Doug were looking for a new way of learning, but what they found was a new way of living. For over sixteen years, their search has been intricately interwoven with the birth and growth of the school.

Many years ago, when our daughter Brooke (now eighteen) was just about pre-school age, my husband Doug saw an ad in the paper for an evening class at Colorado Mountain College about Waldorf Kindergarten. We knew very little about Waldorf education at that time but we were rapidly realizing that exploring educational options was a high priority for us. Together we attended Patty Fox's fascinating, enchanting class, little knowing that our lives were about to change in very exciting and fulfilling ways.

From the beginning we met many Waldorf educators who were devoted, well-spoken, can-do individuals. Doug and I attended our first workshop about Waldorf education with Merlyn and René Querido at Star Mesa near Aspen. Most of the concepts of which René spoke were very new for me but when Merlyn had all of us dancing a five-pointed star to the rhythm of the multiplication table of 5, I felt, "Yes, this is how children should learn!"

The first fundraiser in spring of 1991 was at our house. We were ecstatic when we raised $8,000, even if we later discovered that $6,000 came from Patty's mother-in-law, Pauline Fox, who wanted her grandchildren in a Waldorf School. The mayor, Bill Stirling, attended that event and parked his car blocking traffic. In the middle of the presentation by Eugene Schwartz, in walked two police officers. We feared they were going to shut down the entire event, but they only asked Mayor Bill for his keys.

Our enthusiasm for growing the Waldorf school connected us to an amazing network of Waldorf experts. Eugene Schwartz's lectures on Waldorf education so inspired me that I followed him to the Shepherd Valley Waldorf School in Boulder for a weekend workshop. There I met Jennifer Thompson, an artist and teacher inspired by Rudolf Steiner's ideas. I began to learn about veil painting and curative art work.

The uplifting effect of these painting techniques prompted us to organize painting classes for our community members. In addition to Jennifer Thompson, a host of others were to lead these germinal painting classes, often while they were engaged in helping the school with other matters. Charles Andrade, our Lazure master, Barbara Klocek, kindergarten and art teacher, Patty Doyle, class teacher and veil painter, Helena Hurrell, nurturing arts teacher, Kathryn King, Waldorf development facilitator and Professor of Consciousness Studies, Dennis Klocek, all opened our senses to the world of color through the renewed art of watercolor painting.

Our family soon realized that Waldorf education, so multifaceted in itself, is part of a still bigger picture. We came to understand that our daughter's healthy life in school would be bolstered as we adapted a healthier life style at home. We met anthroposophical doctors like Dr. Philip Incao, whose conventional medical training was expanded and enhanced by further studies of holistic diagnosis and treatment developed by Rudolf Steiner. Their insights helped us understand common phenomena like fever and chills in an entirely new way, while CP Kanipe taught us a great deal about homeopathic remedies. The kindergarten teachers' encouragement to keep the junk food out of our children's lunch boxes led us to learn about the value of healthy organic food, particularly "biodynamic" produce, grown according to principles indicated by Steiner and E. E. Pfeiffer. Before long, the school made efforts to develop its own biodynamic garden, and Keith Schlussler and his wife, Julie McCallan, led study groups on biodynamic gardening. Many school parents labored to comprehend Steiner's *Agriculture* while Keith's handiwork out in the gardens produced massive crops of healthy vegetables.

Our eagerness to share this form of education with the whole world has gotten us into hot water at times. As we completed the construction of the first classrooms at the Roaring Fork campus, we accepted any and every student who came to us, hoping to share the benefits of Waldorf education with everyone and trying to achieve healthier class sizes and a healthier budget. Circumstances taught us the hard way that we had to slow down and learn how to define ourselves as a Waldorf school. Leonore Russell, a teacher and consultant from the Garden City Waldorf School in New York, came to our school to advise us. She led workshops in parent education and conducted meetings with school leaders. She helped us to better explain what new parents are signing up for when they bring their children to the school.

As our parent body expanded beyond its original group of founding pioneers, we realized the need to put policies and procedures down on paper. Our group was too large for us to continue communicating and explaining everything by word of mouth. At this stage of our growth we drew on the experience and expertise of our Waldorf neighbors from Colorado's front range. Robert Schiappacasse and Thom Schaefer from Shining Mountain Waldorf School in Boulder helped us with mentoring programs, a teacher evaluation plan and job descriptions for each sub-group of the school. We learned about running our meetings using principles of consensus from Caroline Estes and Donald Sampson. Most decisions in the world today are not made using a consensus process, so for newcomers to our school this method takes some getting used to. Caroline and Donald helped us learn that at first consensus may appear to be slow and cumbersome. Once a consensus decision is achieved, however, the momentum behind its implementation is considerable.

From the day that we first learned about Waldorf education from Patty Fox, my husband Doug and I found ourselves making a commitment to the physical growth, soul unfolding and spiritual development of the school. As we look back over our past sixteen years of service to the Waldorf School on the Roaring Fork, we realize how inextricably our personal growth and change has been linked to the school's unfolding and development.

Above: Julia Junqguist and Emma Braddy

May our feelings reach to our heart's inmost core
And seek to unite in love with people of like aim,
With those spirits who, full of grace,
Look down on our earnest, heartfelt striving
Sending strength out of regions of light
Bringing light into our love.

Verse for North America
Rudolf Steiner

George Lilly

Oftentimes one small event can alter the life of a community. George midwifed Waldorf ideas for some of the founding parents.

I was introduced to Waldorf education while attending a healing arts festival in Boulder. A veil painting class was offered in addition to workshops on acupuncture, homeopathy, macrobiotics, and other topics for those with an alternative bent. I'd always enjoyed art and found it very exciting to be engaged in the challenge of watercolor painting using a technique of creating veils of color and light. In the workshop I learned that veil painting was an expression of anthroposophical philosophy and part of the Waldorf school curriculum, and it was then that I realized how profound a Waldorf education must be. Although I didn't have children at the time nor was I yet a midwife, I found the concepts of a gentle, developmental approach to learning very compelling.

Several years later, when I was a mother and a midwife, there was not yet a Waldorf school in the valley, so I homeschooled my first two boys until they were ten, using Waldorf principles as a model. I wove art and organic interaction with the earth into our "lessons." When birth clients asked about my thoughts on schooling, I told them about Waldorf education and shared my belief that it seemed to be the best system. CP Kanipe and Karinjo DeVore were among those who asked, and they went on to become two founders of the school. And, as it turned out, as a midwife I caught the baby who became the first and only graduate of the Aspen Waldorf School.

My youngest son, Teva, started school as a first grader in Frances Lewis' class at the Yellow Brick School in Aspen, and his class recited a poem by Alfred, Lord Tennyson at that first graduation for lone graduate Marina Kanipe. I was thrilled that the school had finally manifested and that at least one of my sons would receive a true Waldorf education. He graduated from WSRF in 2004. Now I am the office coordinator at the school and am involved daily with what was once only an inspiration.

"Waldorf ideas steeped in my soul for years."

16

Eugene Schwartz

A Waldorf consultant from the U.S. to Austria, Eugene has graduated three first-through-eighth grades and was a friend to the school from the beginning.

After I gave a talk in 1990, at the inception of the College of Teachers of the Shining Mountain Waldorf School in Boulder, Patty Fox asked if I knew there was a movement afoot to start a Waldorf school in Aspen. She wanted to start not an ordinary private school, but a school that would be aligned with the public schools, a Waldorf alternative. I was extremely skeptical. I didn't think there was enough of a permanent population to support a school, and celebrities moved their children from place to place. Patty insisted that there really were down-to-earth people there and if I would visit I would see that. I told her that if the school was already going and representing Waldorf philosophy, I felt bound to help.

My first "official" meeting in Aspen was with Betsy Hill, principal of the Aspen Middle School. I was astonished at her interest in Waldorf education and her feeling that the possibility of a track in the public school could happen. I knew, having experienced a bit of this in California and New York, that principals and superintendents are often farsighted and even visionary when it comes to Waldorf education but teachers feel threatened by what they might have to change.

In spite of my skepticism and concern that things were happening too quickly, and that demographically a school might not be supported, a seed had been planted in Aspen. It was clear that when these people put their will behind something, it was going to happen. The next year, I came straight into Aspen where something young and vital was happening – sprinkled with fresh powder .

Eugene Schwartz and Patty Fox

Mayfaire celebration at Triangle Park, Aspen, Colorado

I would visit the school and give one or two well-attended evening lectures that put me in touch with the larger community. The audiences were alive, filled with profound questions. They couldn't wait for me to finish a sentence to raise their hands to ask a question. I could see that a Waldorf school here was going to change the lives of many people, some who were in a position to change the tenor of the whole community. The larger community was also being reached through Grassroots TV, radio interviews, and *The Aspen Times*, where I was interviewed. The Aspen

initiative had a high profile, was more grandiose in its goals, more determined.

Every year I would visit there was a little more growth, in spite of occasional negativity from new parents who would come passionately and then drop out for no apparent reason. One felt that though the seed case might be battered and cracked, the kernel within really had integrity. Something was there. More than most, they were FAMILY writ large. Teachers, parents and board members were all the same people, few and tight.

As a Waldorf consultant, I have ties with over 100 schools but I've never seen more strong and vibrant personalities or greater selflessness. These people could have been doing any number of worthy things with their lives, but they devoted themselves to the school by a strong destiny. Year by year it grew more independent, attracting young and vital teachers who made their contributions and stayed or moved on.

I've often had the impression that something of medieval Europe has reincarnated in the Roaring Fork Valley. The "castles" are up on the hillside with the higher view, defending against those who would

invade their way of life. The villagers and craftspeople who tend the land with daily work are in the valley. Who bridged the two in medieval times? The monasteries and the monks who lived in them, the bards and minstrels, and the craftspeople who became the artists. This bridge impulse lives in Waldorf schools. We know that a monastic impulse lives in Waldorf teachers who devote themselves to the education, to beauty and a pathway to the spirit with little compensation. One should never forget the original impulse of the Goethe Bicentennial in Aspen because that is what the Waldorf school really embodies.

Chapter 2

The First 3 Years

This quote hung on the refrigerator of every Aspen Waldorf School founder for years.

Until one is committed, there is hesitancy, the chance to draw back, always ineffectiveness. Concerning all acts of initiative and creation, there is one elementary truth the ignorance of which kills countless ideas and splendid plans: that the moment one definitely commits oneself, then Providence moves, too.

All sorts of things occur to help one that would never otherwise have occurred. A whole stream of events issues from the decision, raising in one's favor all manner of unforeseen incidents and meetings and material assistance, which no man could have dreamed would have come his way.

W. H. Murray

Whatever you can do, or dream you can, begin it. Boldness has genius, power and magic in it. Begin it now.

Wolfgang Goethe

ASPEN WALDORF SCHOOL

The First Year

At Powder Pandas, we swept down a year's worth of cobwebs, draped silk and cotton to soften hard edges, arranged playstands and desks. In two days, the children's ski school was transformed into a sweet Waldorf school. Patty Doyle took firm control of her angelic little class. Applying her Rudolf Steiner College training, her double major in journalism and German at the University of Colorado, and her talents as an artist, musician,

Brooke Sheffer has her face painted to match her Halloween costume

chef and athlete, Patty had the fledg-lings marching after her devotedly, drawing, singing, learning their letters and sums, and playing their melodic pentatonic flutes.

The kindergarten was not so calm. Patty Fox had no experience in a classroom so radically different from public school. CP had no classroom ex-perience at all. When Dana Fordham came to observe, she was graciously horrified and set to work teaching us to apply the three R's of the Waldorf kindergarten: rhythm, ritual and repetition.

Still, we dearly loved our infant school. The board was working hard to raise funds, the parents were pleased, the larger community sup-portive. The christening came on September 29th, a perfect Aspen day with sunlit golden leaves drifting down onto our Michaelmas harvest celebration in the secluded yard. Perhaps forty families, all of our own

Patty Doyle's founding first grade, Winter, 1991

and many guests, pressed apple cider, played games, jumped rope and felt held by the Light.

On the weekend before the first of November, parents, teachers and board members – who were really one and the same – moved us into our rooms in the Yellow Brick School. Again we had to go through the process of cleaning, painting and draping to add beauty. Daniel Olave a carpenter, who came to the school through the Sheffers, began building the desks, tables and chairs still in use today. Our new home felt more

institutional and less homey and we never accommodated ourselves to the heart-wrenching sound of babies crying from the childcare operations that shared the building, but we were happy to have found a home that would be ours for as long as we wanted.

In order to build enrollment and, hopefully, our financial base, we began publishing a newsletter and hosting a public festival each month. We defined ourselves through the newsletter which was written by Patty Fox and designed by Betsy Engelman.

22

The festivals grew larger with every season. Especially memorable was the Valentine's celebration. Inspired by Betsy's handwork, the faculty performed a charming puppet play, *The Bluebird with the Golden Heart*, and Pam Wicks led Valentine's dances. Thirty or forty families often attended our festivals furthering their knowledge of Waldorf education. We learned quickly that festivals didn't immediately fill the coffers or the classes. They did, however, bond our inner community and brought us recognition in the larger one.

We celebrated our baby's first year in Triangle Park, dancing the Maypole with crowns of flowers and ribbon wands. The school was healthy and returning our devoted care with abundant love.

*Oh yes, Mayfaire.
What was the first thing
we had to do to have
a Mayfaire?
Billy Engelman had a
metal sleeve fabricated
that would fit into a tire.
Then we poured
cement into the tire to
hold the Maypole.
That was the first thing.
Then we had to build a
ramp and get three men
to roll the 200 pound tire
into Jim Fox's truck,
haul it to Triangle Park,
roll it out and fit the
decorated pole into it.
Afterwards, we hauled
it back to Fox's barn
to store.
We did that every year.
When we had
the Mayfaire at the
Youth Center,
there were three inches
of new snow. We set the
Maypole up in the plaza
and had to move it into
the Youth Center to do
the dance. Oh, yes.
I remember Mayfaires.*
Stephen Kanipe

The Second Year

Our success the first year encouraged us to repeat summer camp at Windstar. The camp was packed, the parents pleased, the board members and teachers exhausted but happy. It was devastating to learn afterwards that kindergarten teacher Dana Fordham had been diagnosed with cancer of the thymus. The disease was so far advanced that it would take her life a year later, leaving her husband Bill, who had taught the six- and seven-year-olds, with two young boys and our kindergarten with a guardian angel, but no mentor.

School began with a bulging three-day-a-week kindergarten and a slightly enlarged second/third grade. Patty and CP were astounded that even from her sick bed, Dana could offer just the right antidote for any ailment and the kindergarten children thrived. We were quite sure that we'd start a healthy first grade and perhaps two kindergartens the next year. The second and third graders did us proud with their beautiful main lesson books, form drawing and flute performances, class play and Spanish dances.

A racer herself, Patty Doyle takes her second grade class Nordic skiing

Our festivals continued but with less ambitious frequency. In late September, Patty Doyle's class was adorable in *Stone Soup* with kindergarteners bobbing in the soup pot. The Lantern Walk in November included new faces lit by the glow of lanterns as we trudged bravely through knee-deep snow across Main Street and into the gazebo in Paepcke Park, singing lantern songs. In December, the quiet, meditative Advent Walk brought tears to our eyes and peace to our hearts, so grateful were we that the children could experience bringing their light into a darkened world.

In summer, Patty Fox and CP Kanipe left for Rudolf Steiner College to begin their formal Waldorf teacher training. Everyone else sighed with relief that no summer camp or major event was planned.

Patty Fox and CP Kanipe with their kindergarten, 1992

Dana Fordham

The Third Year

The kindergarten teachers returned excited by their training and their new co-teacher from England, Jo Richter. But third years are often uphill climbs and ours was like climbing a fourteen thousand foot peak. Dana left us in August and we scattered her ashes at Windstar, where some of her best memories, and ours, were created. Many still feel her presence as a guardian angel of our school, especially of the kindergartens.

Two weeks before school started and still in mourning, it became apparent that not only were we not going to have new first graders, we were not going to fill even one kindergarten. The faculty of four confronted the future gloomily trying to decide who should resign. Patty Doyle felt pressure from parents expecting more in terms of time allocated for her work. She felt a break might help solve that. Patty Fox and CP were willing, perhaps too willing, to seek other employment.

Finally we saw that Patty Fox could take the third grade class for a year even though it included her daughter, Maureen, and her only Waldorf training was in preparation for kindergarten. Patty Doyle could take a year off to bike around New Zealand with Adam Stopeck and then return if she wanted. We debated, feeling positive about the idea one minute, negative the next. Three days later, with the board's approval, we agreed to the change with painfully mixed emotions. Patty and Patty took the little class for a walk from Maroon Lake to Crater Lake. Patty Doyle told a story about a beautiful garden tended by a young gardener who loved the garden, but had to leave it in the hands of a new but devoted gardener. We all cried. The year began minus one Patty. Patty Fox, CP and Jo took up the work with determination but a loss of innocence. At two, it seemed our school had returned to crawling.

Painting together in third grade, 1993

As is often the case when the going gets rough, help arrives from an expected source, just as our Goethe quote had assured. In the fall, Merlyn and René Querido returned to give lectures and encourage our feeble initiative. They reminded us that Steven Moore, their dear friend, was living in Paonia and might be available as a specialty teacher. When Steven agreed to join the faculty as a speech, drama and eurythmy teacher, we felt honored. He had a twinkle in his eye and a listening ear, years of Waldorf teaching and anthroposophy, and he truly walked his talk. He began teaching once a week, then twice, balancing his work in Aspen with that at the independent Lamborn Valley School in Paonia. He led an adult study and eurythmy group and his thoughtful presence was an anchor during that tumultuous year and for the next decade.

Glenn Engelman, Matt Fox and Tristan Kanipe "hung around" a lot while their mothers worked in the classroom!

Brooke Sheffer learns to hammer

Responsibility for the school was no easier at the board level. Patty Fox continued as president for the third year, but trying to balance enrollment and fund-raising was becoming a full-time job for many parents. The monthly public festivals were reduced to one in fall and one in spring. Pam Moore took charge of a Halloween Journey. The long, dark hall of the Yellow Brick School was aglow with sixty carved pumpkins. Coordinating with other tenants and the Aspen Dance Connection, we transformed three rooms into enchanted enclaves: a crystal cave with chanting gnomes; the wind-swept frozen home of the brave duck, Shingebiss; a forest with dancing trees and knee-deep leaves. Hundreds of families paid $2 to travel the magical lands and we were delighted with the overwhelming community response. Afterwards, we had to admit that the journey had produced only a few hundred dollars and no instant enrollments, but it had brought joy to many children and the pumpkins' glow still warms our hearts.

Josh Altenbernd and Brittany Fortier in the kindergarten, 1994

But how could we go on? Most of our parents were struggling to pay the meager tuition of $3,000 a year. We didn't want to limit our enrollment to only those who could pay a higher price but we couldn't pay our teachers a minimum wage indefinitely. When Colorado adopted the Charter School Initiative, it seemed the perfect solution. If approved, we would receive state funding and, we hoped, maintain the Waldorf curriculum with few concessions. Liz Stewart, Larry Doble, Stephen Kanipe, Marisa Post, Bob Schultz, chairperson and Gary Beach as the vice chairperson, began to explore applications to both the Aspen and Roaring Fork School Districts. The project grew, demanding endless time in public surveys, written proposals, explanations of the curriculum, interviews and presentations. Patty Fox, representing the Waldorf curriculum, realized by late winter that her incomplete Waldorf

Emily helps Melony learn to paint

Mayfaire, 1995

training was not enough to carry the application forward and we had no one else who was better qualified. Without a thoroughly trained teacher, an authority, our application was compromised. She withdrew from the effort, disappointing some, relieving others and fomenting a split of sorts in the board. Doug, Bob and Gary Beach tried to carry through the application but were finally denied by both districts.

The application for a charter made clear the willfulness and petulance of our almost three-year-old school. It could now say, "I" and "No!" but didn't really know what it wanted. We decided we needed an authority, someone who could tell us the right things to do to grow up into a "real Waldorf school." The year ended bit-terly for some, satisfactorily for others, but still joyfully for the children. Jo Richter returned to England, CP left for Rudolf Steiner College again and Patty Fox ventured to Antioch Graduate School in Maine, which offered a masters program in Waldorf education, to begin her class teacher training.

Patty Doyle and her children Avital, Sophie and Finnlay

"I feel grace in the fact that
I had the opportunity to
undertake something of
magnitude in the mountains
I had grown up in."

Patty Doyle

Patty's place, insisted René Querido, was in her hometown of Aspen, helping to found a Waldorf school.

I was first inspired to teach while on a post-graduate program in Germany. Nearly all of my friends there were studying to be teachers – in a country where the profession has some clout. When not in school, I traveled Europe with friends who had been on the Nordic ski team with me at the University of Colorado. Near the end of my travels, I worked on a sheep farm for a couple of months. It was there that I first learned of Waldorf education.

A family on an alternative vacation to this self-sufficient medieval farm captured my attention right away.

The respect that the children had for their parents and that the parents had for the children impressed me. I had never seen a family so clearly content. It turned out that the parents were both teachers at the original Waldorf School in Stuttgart. In the years since then, anthroposophy and Waldorf education have given me so much, but above all I think I have been able to realize the dream of attaining what that family in far-away Europe demonstrated almost twenty years ago: mutual respect between parents and children and the importance of protecting childhood.

I thought I could return to the U.S. and just become a Waldorf teacher but when I called the San Francisco Waldorf School to apply, they chuckled and told me about the two-year teacher training in Sacramento. I met René Querido, the director of Rudolf Steiner College,

Patty and Betsy

Patty took her adoring class Nordic skiing at Pine Creek Cookhouse when she returned from New Zealand, 1994.

Patty teaching her first class, 1992

while home in Aspen and enrolled immediately. Within a month, I decided I must leave. So much of what was said was at odds with all of my previous ideas. But I stayed one day too long! Waldorf education had me. I shall never unlearn what I learned there (as much as I would like to sometimes; this stuff is so counter-culture!) and when René pressured me to come back to Aspen to start the new school, I did.

I devoted myself to that first class of nine children. It has been one of my greatest joys to watch them grow and become commendable young adults. In Waldorf schools, the class teacher is responsible for the two-hour main lesson and some additional lessons, but not the whole day. For the first two years, the only specialty teacher we had was Betsy Engelman for handwork. I spent the rest of the day alone with my class teaching them every specialty subject: vocal and recorder music, painting and drawing, games, beeswax modeling and German. Welcome to a pioneering school and thank God for Betsy!

After leaving my first class in Patty Fox's hands, I returned the fourth year of the school to start a new combined first/second grade. After two years with my second class, my husband Adam and I moved to Sacramento so that he could enroll in the two-year teacher training and I could deepen my artistic and Goethean studies. We returned to the Waldorf School on the Roaring Fork in 1999, when Adam took the first grade. I continued to work at the school in various capacities, in between bearing our three children. That school was my whole life and I loved it. I was naïve enough to think that the end of my story there would continue to have humor, even levity, but sadly, it was not our place. A conflicted ending, like mine, is perhaps a karmic consequence of the intensity of the relationships among students, parents and faculty. Still, I feel grace in the fact that I had the opportunity to undertake something of magnitude in the mountains I had grown up in and still love.

Teaching English. As with all aspects of the curriculum, the language arts curriculum adheres to Steiner's view that child development recapitulates the changes in human consciousness through the ages. Language, we know, began orally with stories of the marvels of human experience. Fairy tales, shared by all the world's cultures, are the distillation of these marvels. They symbolically characterize every aspect of the human psyche, rewarding the good and punishing the bad. Communication in writing and reading came much later, presumably beginning with simple symbols that related to the natural world. The complexities of phonics, spelling, grammar and composition developed relatively recently.

Each child's mother tongue is still learned orally in the lullabies, poems, stories and daily communications of the home. Lucky are the children who learn from the human voices around them rather than from digital recordings. Waldorf teachers discourage television, CDs, tapes and videos for all young children because, at the very least, recorded sound compromises both the child's language development and his imagination.

When children enroll in a Waldorf preschool/kindergarten, the wealth of the world's fairy tales is brought to them by their teachers who learn each tale they tell "by heart." Day after day, the children feast with bright eyes and mouths dropped open, drinking in the archetypal symbolic images of these stories which are repeated daily for two or three weeks. The children never tire of them, and when they see them performed as puppet plays or, led by their teachers, act them out themselves, the rich language of these ancient stories pours out of them. Parents are astounded to hear their children retell, at home, the story they have heard at school, word for beautiful word.

The fairy tales continue in first grade, but now, writing is added. Although most children recognize the letters of the alphabet before they start school, the symbols are mysterious scratchings on the page which they love to draw over and over. When they hear the tale of, for example, *The Fisherman and his Wife*, and then draw *F* as a fish, the scratchings acquire deep, personal meaning; they know the letters with their hearts as well as their hands and heads. This personal relationship is furthered when they move the letters in speech eurythmy. At first, the movements for letters are not identified, though the children may "know" them in a deeper sense. In the middle school, when the students learn to "spell" using the movements they learned in the early grades, language expands into a new dimension.

Mufaro's Beautiful Daughters, a puppet play with marionettes created by the seventh/eighth grade

Phonics and word configuration exercises accompany the introduction of the letters. As vocabularies grow, reading emerges from the children's writing. Some children can read their main lesson books from cover to cover during first grade and progress rapidly to other texts. Others are ready in second or even third. They are not rushed. Steiner schools respect individual differences in development and teachers are trained to assess a variety of behaviors before suggesting to parents that special needs may account for delayed reading. When such recommendations are made, thorough assessments for parents and/or specialists support the child's progress.

Beginning with the fairy tales in first grade, animal fables and stories of the saints in second, and Old Testament stories in third, the children fill their main lessons books with pictures and stories copied from the board and read together. Children's classics such as *Frog and Toad* are introduced as the children progress and they practice their reading several times each day. By the end of third grade, most children are reading fluently. From fourth grade on, the students read from the wide range of old and modern classics. Some, such as *The Second Mrs. Giaconda*, complement the history curriculum; some, *The Yearling*, are chosen to support inner development; and some, *Jane Eyre*, for artistic merit.

The first graders draw their new letter friends carefully and beautifully, one by one, into their main lesson books. They copy a word, then a simple sentence from the board using the letters. While the consonants are introduced as nouns, naming words, the vowels sounds come with feelings: *Ah* (awe) opens to the world in wonder; *A* (acorn) stands back a bit and waits to see what might happen; *E* (enough) stands tall and straight; *O* (open) has an embracing, loving feeling; *U* (unite) joins things together. It is hoped that with this introduction, language will always be a personal treasure to be guarded and preserved.

By fourth grade, the dreaminess of early childhood has come to an end and children are ready to engage as individuals. Grammar and composition, which have been learned through imitation for the first three grades, are now brought to consciousness. To learn composition, the class may generate a retelling and recording of a Norse myth as a group; children may take turns composing sentences; the teacher may start a paragraph and have the children complete it. With each entry into the main lesson book, the children acquire new skills in organization, word choice, dramatic emphasis, spelling and punctuation. In grammar, the four main parts of speech – nouns, verbs, adjectives and adverbs – may be given colorful personalities, much as the four arithmetic operations of adding, subtracting, multiplying and dividing are. Again, artistic exercises reinforce this new learning and are practiced and expanded into all parts of speech. Sentences may be diagrammed using several techniques.

The middle school curriculum includes reading and writing poetry and short stories, research and book reports, and business and personal letters. The students may write scripts to accompany puppet plays or skits for their monthly assemblies. In each grade, in each setting, the language arts program at the Waldorf School on the Roaring Fork strives to respect THE WORD, the most precious resource of all human experience.

Foreign language instruction is another hallmark of Waldorf schools. Ideally, two modern foreign languages are introduced in first grade with at least an introduction to Greek and Latin in the upper grades. While the Waldorf School on the Roaring Fork has yet to achieve this ideal, they have offered Spanish and German at different times and currently have a well-grounded Spanish program in place.

The foreign language curriculum follows closely the language arts program outlined above. Just as the child learns his mother tongue orally by imitating songs, stories and names, the foreign language teacher begins with nursery rhymes, poems and naming games with a musical quality, allowing the children in the first three grades to develop a large vocabulary before the rules of the new language are learned. The flexibility of the tongue, innate in young children, is maintained through an oral approach and it may be argued that this oral flexibility supports mental flexibility as well.

The festivals and customs of the countries where the foreign language is spoken enliven the lessons in all of the grades. By third grade, children's classics in the language expand reading beyond the resources of the children's own lesson books and by fourth grade, grammar rules are introduced, noun-verb agreement is explained and conjugation of verbs is practiced. The lessons in the upper grades continue with conversations, composition, reading and grammar, and each level of mastery results not only in a better understanding of the foreign language and culture but also, a better understanding of our own.

Billy Engelman, Tim Fortier and Jim Fox brought down to earth the dreams of their wives and the board: demonstrated most dramatically when they became "the sod fathers," laying an acre of sod three days before the school opened in Carbondale. *See page 87.*

Pam Wicks

Pam brought her familiarity with eurythmy and music to the Aspen Waldorf School.

I learned about Waldorf in the late 60's when, living in London, I went to the school of eurythmy to buy a piano. I was in my early 20's, the awakening of my consciousness, and reading Jung, Dostoyevsky, Hesse. When I heard about Steiner's work at the eurythmy school, I went straight to the Goetheanum in Dornach, Switzerland, the center for Rudolf Steiner's philosophy, to learn more. I was reading *The Glass Bead Game* at the time and when I saw that curvaceous architecture and listened to the people there, I thought, "I'm in this book!"

I returned to Montreal and met hard-core, rigid German anthroposophic mystics there. They were insular, but wonderful. My next encounter was as an accompanist for Owen, a big, masculine, good-looking young eurythmy teacher at the Lexington Waldorf School near Boston. When he came leaping in with his eurythmy slippers on, it was a hoot. We became colleagues as I learned to create improvisations on the piano for his fairies, gnomes and giants. I still use these themes with my storytelling.

Ted and I married and when Sierra (Cici) was born, I shared my thoughts on Waldorf. It was too weird for him. He needed to see a mature, established school to believe in it and I didn't show him one. Nonetheless, when I heard from my friend Eleanor Jacobs that a Waldorf school was in the plan-

Pam Wicks on guitar, Patty Doyle, Josephine Mann and Stephen Kanipe on recorder and drums – our Mayfaire band, 1992

ning stages in Aspen, I joined the effort. In those early years, we were all so willing to give life to the new school! Leaving the house in a snowstorm in the middle of winter to drive fifteen miles to a board meeting, I was joyful. I taught the board members songs and canons with which we'd start or end our meetings: "Rise up oh flame, by thy light shining, bring to us beauty, vision and joy." And I remember

our verse to close: "Life grows more radiant about me / Life grows more arduous for me / Life grows more abundant within me." We felt the words and the spirit of our community so deeply. Barbara Allen brought coffee and tea and treats. I cherish the memories of those early days when we had the innocence of children, though I guess we also needed the struggles for the school to find form.

When the school began, Sierra was in the kindergarten. I led the music for our monthly festivals and class plays. By the third year, Skye was in the kindergarten and I was teaching vocal music and recorder. I loved bringing Native American songs to the third grade to go along with their house (and teepee) building block. But by then, Ted was pulling me away. We compromised by sending the girls to the Aspen Community School until we moved to California but I'm still a Waldorf person through and through. I've followed every detail of the school's development through Eleanor and believe that even in the two or three years they were there, my girls took something special from it. Perhaps they've come full circle. They're in Millbrook School in New York now, the private school their grandfather founded, and although it looks like a prep school, it is really "head, heart and hands" like a Waldorf school.

"Leaving the house in a snowstorm in the middle of winter to drive fifteen miles to a board meeting, I was joyful."

CP Kanipe

CP was a founder, the first kindergarten assistant and a teacher for seven years.

When I moved to Aspen in 1976, I worked at the Little Kitchen Restaurant where the local hippies hung out. Many of them later found their way to the Waldorf school. When Marina was in the public kindergarten, every day the school nurse called to say she was complaining of a stomach ache. Even though she was getting rave reviews from her teachers, the day came when she wouldn't go to school. I began home-schooling her using the Oak Meadow curriculum that is inspired by Waldorf methods. Although I didn't attend the earliest Waldorf gatherings, I knew I'd enroll my children if there was a Waldorf school. In fall of 1990 though, Patty Fox ran into me at City Market, handed me the flier for her CMC class and said I should sign up – today! I did. I was thrilled to be able to learn more about the curriculum as no one else in the upper valley was home-schooling then.

Stephen and I began attending meetings with the school board and became involved with summer camp. Marina loved her camp with Patty Doyle but when the school opened that fall with a combined first/second grade, she was already a third grader and was sure that she'd be behind her peers if she didn't attend public school. She soon found that she wasn't behind at all and she missed the Waldorf friends and methods she'd experienced. The next year she joined the second grade class as a fourth grader and we supplemented at home with the stories she should have been learning to try to meet her inner development. When she graduated from the sixth grade curriculum to start at Aspen High School, the only graduate of the Aspen Waldorf School, she had six hard weeks – followed by four years on the honor roll.

Our kindergarten teacher had backed out just before we opened the school and I'd agreed to assist Patty Fox with the kindergarten – but only until Thanksgiving, when my massage business picked up. I never left. For two years we just kept trying to do as Dana Fordham taught us. By the second year, the kindergarten was full. Patty and I went off to Rudolf Steiner College sure that everyone in the Aspen community now realized what a great school Waldorf was and would want to join us, but we were wrong. Aspen never did join.

Patty and I had a fabulous introduction to the training and laughed ourselves to the verge of hysteria living in "Daisy," the small RV Patty borrowed from her parents. But when we came home with Jo Richter as a third kindergarten teacher, the reality was sobering. Patty Fox replaced Patty Doyle in the third grade and Jo Richter and I struggled with an under-enrolled kindergarten. Parents who had known me from the Little Kitchen found it hard to believe that I now knew something they didn't about child development.

The next year, when I returned from further training at RSC, I found that my new assistant, Barbara Allen, had spent the greater part of her summer creating a sweet, rosy kindergarten room from one that ART-C, the theater group, had painted black. I'll always be grateful to Barbara for her dedication – and the snacks and lovely handwork for which she became famous.

"If we really knew what we were taking on – if we truly had any idea what 'starting a school' meant – would we have done it?"

When the school moved, I stepped out of teaching, but chaperoned the bus, volunteered in the office and substituted. When the school stood at a critical juncture in 1999, the near-desperate faculty twisted my arm to come back to the kindergarten. It was a wonderful year, the first year when I felt truly supported by parents and faculty. Although we were still feeling the effects of our nine-year change, we wanted to move forward.

Many times I've asked myself, "If we really knew what we were taking on – if we truly had any idea of what 'starting a school' meant – would we have done it?" Fourteen years later I can say, "Yes!" I will never be the same – and that's the good news!

Pam Moore

Pam, a school founder, struggled with the education before coming to peace with it.

My friend Karinjo DeVore introduced me to Waldorf education. When my first child Keegan was two, we planned to attend a workshop being taught by Steven Moore, Nancy Poer and Merlyn and René Querido at the Shining Mountain Waldorf School in Boulder. Karinjo couldn't go so I went with our shared babysitter, Mindy, with the goal of getting her to turn off the TV. At the workshop, we learned not only why turning off the television was a good idea but also ways to fill our children's days with creative opportunities.

Although I had helped with events before the Waldorf school opened, I was wary of launching a school. I enrolled Keegan in the Aspen Community School for kindergarten and first grade but found that the many choices that she was given by her teachers wore her out. As I read and learned more about Waldorf education, I came to understand that a child doesn't need to be presented with endless choices but rather needs guidance from parents and teachers. Keegan entered the Waldorf school in second grade and Stella started in preschool. That year I was in charge of the first and only Halloween Journey in Aspen. We transformed the school building I'd attended as a child into an imaginative child's world and it was magical, a high point of fantasy.

Following Patty Fox's lead, I then carried on with the organization of the Mayfaire and Winterfaire festivals, two events that have become traditional in our school calendar.

I loved being part of the community movement, learning, questioning and struggling with many tenets of Waldorf curriculum. As Rudolf Steiner insists in *How to Know Higher Worlds* it is important that we question concepts until we know them

> *"The breadth and depth of the history curriculum – the story of human beings – is the best part for me. Eleanor of Aquitaine lives in Stella; Perseus lives in Keegan. We are each unique individuals but we are carrying the whole story of humankind. After hearing those hundreds of stories, Keegan and Stella have a rare concept of what makes a human being human."*

to be true ourselves. An example of my education was the parents' painting class taught by Kathryn King. At the time I was questioning why we (and the children) painted the same picture as the teacher. Each week opened my eyes to the subtle differences in our perception of the same subject and in the magic of merging water and pigment. I learned not only about colors, but

Barbi and Pam at Mayfaire, 1998

about my friends as well. Our pictures were not the same. In a Waldorf school there are spheres within spheres: the parent body, the teacher body, the board, the physical body, the etheric body, the astral body and the ego. We dance in a multidimensional way, trying to understand, but everyone hung in there and so far, I've always come to terms with Steiner's indications.

In spite of my dedication to the ideals of Waldorf education, I was taken aback when the school hired Frances Lewis to be Stella's teacher. She was young, still in training and was joining a school that was itself still young. Would she receive the guidance and help that she would need to educate my daughter? I enrolled my daughters in public school but after two weeks, I recognized that I needed to trust the school's judgment and I brought my girls back to the Waldorf setting. In time, I realized what a gift from on high Miss Lewis was. I watched that young girl grow into a woman and saw her as a shining star guiding our children. She was really called to teach in a Waldorf school.

The cultivation of values is essential to the survival of humankind. Empty gestures deny values. The days I spent helping to build the buildings of our new campus make up some of my most precious

memories. The magic of helping to found the school gave many roles to many people; the school also formed the people. Over the years, we had many meetings filled with frustrations, super-sized personalities and intense politics. Waldorf education attracts strong, idealistic individuals and making it work calls for a group process. I learned that I am an "idea person," one who can work hard in short bursts, better suited to organize a festival than to sit through board meetings. Therefore, this endeavor has been the most fulfilling adventure of my life. Now, seeing my younger sister Valery at the school with her baby and our mom, I see that the school will bridge generations. The valley residents who graduated from the Waldorf school will send their children to the school. In a valley known for ceaseless change, the Waldorf school will endure for a long, long time.

Halloween Journey, 1993

History

From Distant Past to Present and from Infant to Adult

In the first grade, the fairy tales are chosen to introduce the letters of the alphabet and to generate original sentences for the children to write and begin reading. Why fairy tales? A key to understanding the Waldorf curriculum is Steiner's contention that humans, as they grow from infancy to adulthood, recapitulate changing human consciousness from the most distant past to the present. At each stage of development there are moods, myths, events and individuals that meet the inner being of the growing child, beginning with prehistory in first grade and ending with the morning paper in high school.

The still dreamy mood of the young child is found in the fairy tales. In kindergarten and first grade, the children listen to the stories, open-mouthed and absorbed. As modern psychology – Jung's collective consciousness, for example – has illuminated, the fairy tales embody all aspects of the human psyche from wicked stepmother to wise woman, princess to crone, rascal to prince, and simpleton to king. And always, the good overcomes the bad. Fairy tales have been the moral training ground for children for millennia and (though sometimes altered by modern media) can still be so.

By second grade, children begin to feel their individuality more keenly. They are not so willing to listen open-mouthed to their beloved teacher. They need to be able to laugh at themselves when they are naughty tricksters and they need real heroes to emulate. Animal fables and stories of saints provide these contrasts.

At some point between eight and ten, every child treads the difficult nine-year change, a passage leading away from the paradise of early childhood. Santa Claus and the Easter Bunny aren't real; cruel people and sad events must be met. For western civilization, for Jews, Christians and Muslims, the stories of the Old Testament are a depiction of this time. God casts Adam and Eve from the Garden so that they must work in the world. Their food no longer falls from the trees; they must plow and sow and harvest. Life on earth is not eternal; we grow old, suffer and die. Yet God continues to guide his children. Good works, patience and fortitude are rewarded and life has new meaning. Third graders study the Old Testament, farming and earth measurement. They build model houses and deepen their modern survival skills of reading, writing and arithmetic. Human consciousness meets the demand of living on the earth.

And then come the Norse myths, such powerful stories that the children weep at Ragnarok, the Twilight of the Gods. They ponder the story of Askr and Embla who survive to hear Yggdrasil, the world ash tree, whisper, "Look at me and you will see yourselves." This image of Yggdrasil will serve for the multitude of stories told in the fourth grade, for Yggdrasil translates as "the bearer of the ego," the "I." Through the story of Yggdrasil, who is nourished by three sources – the root of ice-cold thinking; the strength and might of giants, the will; and the heart-felt feelings of our moral convictions – the ten-year-old child receives a vibrant picture of the awakening ego.

Now the child is prepared for the wondrous history of civilization and the ongoing human struggle for meaning and for dominion by the ego over the lower nature. Fifth grade history is a magic carpet ride beginning with the dreamy stories of ancient India, the *Ramayana* and *Bhagavat-gita*, and then flying on to Persia and Ahura Mazda's gift of the plow. The Mesopotamians, their stories written on clay tablets, share their lives and struggles with us in *Gilgamesh*. Egyptian hieroglyphs and pyramids, mystery schools and preparations for death further intrigue the students.

With the Greeks, the new impulse of independent, individualized thinking enters the world. Greek history might begin with the story of Pallas Athena springing from the head of Zeus, armed with metal but also with cunning and strategy, with thinking. It is Athena who enables the divergent city-states of Greece to win the Trojan War and defeat a million invading Persians. It is thinking that leads to the birth of philosophy, poetry, architecture, drama, sculpture and the sciences, the foundations of civilization on which we stand today. Botany, zoology, astronomy, chemistry and physics, which the fifth through eighth grade students will be studying, all descend from Greek roots.

In this grand tour, teachers present different ways of looking at the world. In the *Bhagavad-gita*, we find the phrase, "What is death? It is the discarding of an old coat. And what is birth? It is putting on a new coat," a phrase that can only be understood if the student learns the concepts of karma and reincarnation. By contrast, the Greeks say, "It is better to be a beggar on the earth, than a king in the realm of the shades," questioning reincarnation and the afterlife.

In sixth grade, when students are growing rapidly, the Greek concept of separation of body and soul is introduced. They feel themselves as something beyond their bodies, sometimes even at odds with the behavior of their bodies. They come to understand the roots of the Judaic and Christian religions in which body, soul and spirit are not inseparable.

41

From Plutarch on, biography, the writing of a life, provides the core of the history curriculum. Sixth grade students identify with Julius Caesar or Hannibal and ask, "What is the source of modern ideas? Are these people so different from me?" They conclude that individuality and independent thinking were born in ancient times. When Julius Caesar defies the Senators and crosses the Rubicon, they understand that Romans were "modern" men and women; they felt their lives were determined not by the fates but by themselves.

By the sixteenth century (and seventh grade), no one else could hear the divine spirits of Michael or Marguerite who spoke only to Joan of Arc, yet her impulse led to the division of France and England into independent nations. As national consciousness developed, new ways of thinking were explored by navigators circling the globe and by archeologists uncovering Greek and Roman artifacts. These explorations provided the inspiration for the Renaissance, a new birth in painting, architecture, philosophy and mathematics.

The portrait and self-portrait expressed individuality and originality. Eleanor of Aquitaine inaugurated courtly behavior that raised the status of women, the arts and music. Luther and Calvin initiated the Reformation, a form of self-expression in religion, and insisted on the right to interpret the Bible in their own ways, free from papal influence. Erasmus emphasized human affairs over the natural world or religion. As Europe was torn by upheavals in religion and class structure, many fled to the new world.

The tumultuous teen years are well met by this curriculum. Teenagers too must search their individuality for new ideals and new truths. They become fiercely engaged with friends, or fiercely alone. They resonate with the cries of the revolutionists: "Liberty, Equality and Fraternity!" "Give me liberty or give me death!" Beethoven's First Symphony in 1800 opens with a note of discord and the old forms are broken. His Ninth Symphony closes with the human voice singing, "We are brothers."

The idealism of the revolutions in Europe and America are answered differently in each country and the seeds of later dissension are sown. Eighth graders study the Napoleonic Wars, the American Civil War, and the achievements and human sacrifices resulting from the Industrial Revolution. They are introduced to forms of government born from the revolutions: republic, democracy, oligarchy, monarchy and dictatorship. Economic systems are explored: free enterprise, socialism and communism. The World Wars and later events will be confronted in high school, but a solid foundation has been laid. From mythical beginnings to modern times, the threads of human endeavor are inextricably woven into each human life and yet each of us brings something unique to the earth.

"The process of learning history through stories has created, for me, a colorful, vibrant, three-dimensional picture of the world as it was and as it is now."

Maureen Fox, graduate

Anthia (Tia) Muñoz

43

Eleanor Jacobs

There was never a more willing and enthusiastic founder than Eleanor.

After college, I worked as a teacher's aide and taught some PE classes at Bird Rock Elementary School in La Jolla. I was horrified by public education. I saw one teacher in particular destroy a child's educational success and I remember a kindergarten girl who was so absorbed in reading, so serious and so pushed by her parents, that it seemed she had already lost her childhood. It made me very sad. I didn't want my children to come out of such a mold. I was certain then that I would never send my child to a public school. Of course, at the time I was a little radical myself.

I knew nothing about Waldorf education. But I knew Patty Fox and when she became excited about it and shared information with me, I thought, "This is it! This is what I want for my children." My oldest daughter Emily had been artistic from the time she was very young and the arts were all taught at Waldorf. We weren't musicians at home and when I learned my two girls would be able to sing and play instruments I thought, "How could you not send your child to such a school?" Too, the curriculum was rich in stories of ancient civilizations that were connected to the development of humankind.

The more I heard about the underlying spiritual basis of the education, the more convinced I became. I took Patty's CMC class to educate myself and after that, we were all so brave, we opened the school. I was on the board of trustees – but then, we all were. Whatever needed doing we all said, "I'll do that! I'll do that!" In those first years, there was much to do with speakers and festivals. The parent education was excellent. Joan Condon came, Eugene Schwartz, Betty Staley. When René Querido spoke, he brought tears to my eyes. After the second summer camp, Bill Fordham began an anthroposophical study group on biography that was insightful and spiritually uplifting.

My philosophy of education for little ones was turned upside down when Isabelle started as the youngest kindergartener. Pre-Waldorf, I had wanted to open up Emily's head and pour in everything that she could learn. She watched PBS programs so she'd "know" more.

Eleanor helped chaperone the Colorado history and Boulder pentathlon trip with Emily's class in 1996.

Isabelle's early learning was completely different. That first year, I sold my businesses, Kidding Around and Cheap Shots, divorced, and moved to Basalt. There we didn't have a TV and we read chapter books every night. Emily had learned to read on her own in kindergarten but when Isabelle started reading in second grade, it was truly magical. She fell asleep with *Frog and Toad* under her pillow and awoke in the morning to read some more. She was so excited.

There was lots of fund-raising. I was in charge of flower sales and garage sales and I organized the Mayfaire when it was in downtown Basalt. I'll never forget that Halloween Journey in the Yellow Brick. But always, we struggled with enrollment. It was tough to put on all those events and not have new enrollment. When the property in Carbondale showed itself we already knew that to grow our school, we had to move to the mid-valley.

The move to Carbondale and our beautiful facilities helped draw new families. Kathryn King, our administrator at the time, worked hard on community outreach and parent education. Julie Mulcahy, Nancy Hilty and I, and other devoted parents, worked diligently on enrollment by developing early childhood and parent and tot programs. Only in 2005 did enrollment come to fruition after all of our sweat and heart-felt work. When I saw the list of new first graders at the end of that summer, with eighteen children on it, I sobbed tears of joy. Now you have to make a reservation two months in advance to attend the observation mornings!

Teachers came and teachers went. Frances Lewis was the only teacher to shepherd a class from first through eighth grade and Isabelle had the honor and privilege to be led through childhood into adolescence by this healthy, bright young adult who was wholly devoted to Waldorf. I've never been a spokesperson for Waldorf – it's not my nature to talk a lot – but for fourteen years I've worked, slept and dreamed Waldorf education. I'm grateful for the educational foundation in instrumental music, singing, art, movement and soulful learning my girls have received. They're the best spokespeople for Waldorf now. I'm grateful, too, for my community of friends from the Waldorf School. A great bond still holds us together.

Lisa and Tim Fortier

The Fortiers were always there,
helping to do what needed to be done.

"I worked on all of the festivals; we all did. After all, there were only five or six of us."

Melinda Engelman and our oldest daughter, Alexandra, knew each other at three. Even then Betsy talked to me about Waldorf education. It sounded better than any other option. We were not looking forward to public school for our kids. It's so predictable; it hasn't changed since we were there. Every Waldorf parent says they wish they'd had a school like that, where you'd be praised as much for a woodworking project as for a spelling test and we definitely feel that way. I'm sure that Alexandra is in architecture now at the University of Colorado because of form drawing. Brittany is playing basketball at Aspen High School and when the team travels, lots of the kids knit and crochet. It's very "in." But when they get in trouble, Brittany shows them how to cast on or off and fix their mistakes. Her teammates think that's pretty cool – and so does she.

Lisa: When Betsy, Patty and Karinjo started putting together talks with teachers from Denver, Ina Jaenig and Joan Condon, I liked what they said. I started helping out and then the spring before the girls started kindergarten, we hosted a talk at the Aspen Center for Environmental Studies with Eugene Schwartz. There were probably 150 people there! It was so hopeful and I was so excited, sure we'd get the school started that fall. We didn't and we sent our kindergarteners to the public school. The next summer, Linda Lallier and I worked together at Windstar getting ready for camp. We formed a board that fall, and when I didn't show up one time, I was elected secretary. I worked on all of the festivals; we all did. After all, there were only five or six of us. I stayed on the board for years and helped find the land for the new school.

Tim: The hardest thing for us was that there was too much silence in the administration, especially about money. That, and the fact that no one person was in charge who would say "yes" or "no." I guess politics always has closed-door meetings but it seemed there were a lot of decisions that no one was responsible for. Maybe that had something to do with how long the school took to really get going. Now, there are lots of new people who are really happy to be there. We are, too. We tried putting Joey in the public kindergarten but we just couldn't take it. He's so happy to be at Waldorf.

A Teacher's View of the Handwork Curriculum

By Jill Scher

The hands are the primary instrument that growing children use to inform themselves about the world. What the hand feels, the brain knows. Handwork has been part of the Waldorf curriculum since its inception because it plays such an important function in establishing and activating pathways in the brain, in developing the will of the child, and in fostering self-esteem and an appreciation for beauty.

In first grade, the children come to us wide-eyed. Everything is magical and full of wonder. I begin the year with a small sewing project, a felt mouse or bunny, a project that goes quickly and gives them a chance to learn the routine in class and become familiar with their new teachers. Then they have a little friend to play with when they finish! Next we make our knitting needles, sanding and waxing the dowels. Knitting is the primary activity in first grade because it uses both hands equally to create the left-right brain connection, it requires crossing the mid-line and it moves from left to right in a continuous long thread that emulates learning to read. We teach them a verse so they remember the motions needed to knit correctly:

In through the front door,
Run around the back,
Peek through the window,
And off jumps Jack!

The first grade projects are small squares that can be folded and sewn into a chicken or a butterfly. In second grade, the children knit and purl a striped flute case. When they learn to increase and decrease, they make knitted animals or gnomes, more new friends that require shaping and sewing.

The children study farming and house-building in third grade and so we teach the more active work of spinning, natural dyeing and crochet. They card raw wool on drum or hand carders to prepare it for spinning and learn to spin using drop spindles. We dye their length of yarn with natural dyes and it is used as a stripe in their crocheted hats. Most of the year is

spent in mastering crochet, which can be challenging, but the ability to create a round object that moves outward in a balanced rhythm helps ground the children through the nine-year-change. Spinning and crochet require the use of the will to overcome frustration and mastering these activities gives the children a great sense of accomplishment.

The curriculum turns to sewing, embroidery and cross-stitch in the fourth grade. The children are asked to use more precision in their work and to begin to express their individuality. Their first project is a bag to hold their handwork projects. It is hand-sewn and embroidered with a symmetrical form drawing that includes their initials. There is a harmonious feeling in the room during this project as the children bend industriously over their embroidery and eagerly sew up the side seams.

In early spring we introduce cross-stitch which requires even more exactness. The students create a symmetric design from an abstract watercolor that must be mirrored both top to bottom and side to side. It takes real care for the students to transfer their design from paper to cloth without making mistakes and then cross-stitch it into a needle or pencil case. The emphasis on symmetry in fourth grade is an internal exercise for the children, who are asked to see two sides of something.

Fifth grade brings the students back to knitting, but at an intellectual level. We knit a pair of socks on four needles, learning to knit ribbing and shape the sock to fit the foot. The demanding, mathematical process meets their development with periods of easy, rhythmical knitting that allow for social sharing, and periods of complex increasing and decreasing of stitches where they have to concentrate. A few of the children take to this project right away and zoom through, but most need to work diligently to finish it during the year. This is the last year that knitting is part of the regular curriculum.

We begin sixth grade by felting slippers – making first a plastic pattern from their own feet, then wrapping and wet-felting the slippers to make them strong enough to withstand abrasive treatment. The slippers are then cut off the pattern and felted to the students' feet for final forming. Social issues and chatter can dominate handwork at this age but the students must stay focused if their project is to turn out successfully, a hard-learned lesson for some. Finally the students cut out and sew on leather for soles and they may embellish the slippers with embroidery or bead-work.

During the second half of the year, we make stuffed animals. This work comes as they approach adolescence, a time when students often experience inner turmoil. The animal project requires artistry in the drawing of their chosen animal, will forces in the craftsmanship and execution of it, and imagination in creating and ensouling the animal. The sixth grader is often half in and half out of childhood and the animal project offers comfort and companionship in the midst of confusion.

In seventh grade, the students make either marionettes or dolls, an undertaking which requires the whole year and deepens their experience of their own transforming bodies. The figures are entirely hand-sewn, beginning with the formation of the head. The students who choose dolls form bones (tightly wrapped wool) and painstakingly create the outer form. When the doll is finished, they design and make clothes. With mari-

onettes, an alternate but equally involved project, the human form is not as actualized as with dolls. But they give the students an opportunity to individualize hairstyles and clothing and the added dimension of staging and performing a play.

The eighth grade curriculum focuses on the American, French, Russian and Industrial Revolutions. The students build on what they have learned, with a sewing machine as the tool of choice. After knitting socks, creating patterns for slippers, and hand-sewing clothes for their dolls, they are ready to tackle the mystery of designing and making clothes for themselves. This process takes half the year. The other half is used to explore fabric design techniques such as batik or tie dyeing. By the end of the eighth grade, the students have a good grounding in textile arts but more importantly, they have learned perseverance, an appreciation of beauty, and the satisfaction that comes from creating with their hands.

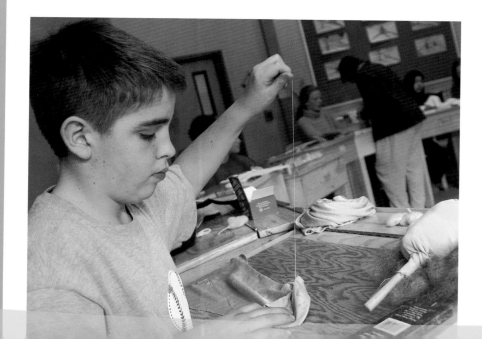

Daniel Olave

Daniel built the furniture for the children.

When I came from my home in Chihuahua, Mexico, I worked for Barbi and Doug Sheffer. When the school started, there was no furniture for it and so Doug and I designed chairs. The first year I made thirty chairs and have made more than a hundred since. Then I made tables that were used in the kindergarten and in the grades. I started making desks in the third year, the single-hinged style. As the children grew, I added spacers to the legs and now those desks are used for the oldest children. I began making the flat double desks after the school moved to Carbondale because the classes grew and the single desks took up too much room and were too heavy for the young children to move. I'm still making and repairing the same models of chairs, desks and tables that we started with and the school keeps growing and needing more.

I think the Waldorf way of studying is very interesting and have always been impressed with the conduct of the students, their discipline. I have never seen a bad child here. I hoped my son would be able to attend this school but after three months in the kindergarten, he felt uncomfortable. There are no other Latinos here, no one to speak Spanish with, and all of his friends are in New Castle.

I would like the school to do more to invite Latinos in. Announcements on the radio, workshops for children and adults, and signs on the road announcing our festivals in Spanish would make them feel welcome. There are many Waldorf books published in Spanish and a study group using them would help Latinos to understand the value of the education.

"When the school started, there was no furniture for it and so Doug and I designed chairs."

Chapter 3

The Forest Floor

Four to Seven

The summer after our third year, we received a call from Kathryn King, a former specialty teacher at the Austin (Texas) Waldorf School. Kathryn, in town visiting friends, had graduated from the Detroit teacher training, a four-year study, and had taught eurythmy for six years. She had left teaching to work in France but was now returning to the U.S. We hoped she would be the authority we thought we needed and when she agreed to join our faculty as a development director, publicizing the school and raising much-needed funds, our anxiety was relieved.

Still, the school was in jeopardy and informational meetings up and down the valley yielded few new enrollments. It was a stunning surprise when the school received an anonymous grant of $100,000 with the promise that we would receive the same amount for five years. We all rejoiced but Eugene Schwartz, our devoted advisor from New York said, "Give it back. You're too young to know what to do with it." Perhaps he was right, but we wouldn't, couldn't listen. The need and temptation were too great.

Patty Doyle returned to us to begin the first new class since our birth, a combined first/second grade. Patty Fox continued with the lead class, a "fourth grade" now composed of one third grader, six fourth graders, one fifth grader, and even one sixth grader. There were bumps. Faculty changes are like re-marriages and require trust in new leadership and new directions; the "mother" and "father" do not always agree.

But we progressed. Christy Braeger began driving children from as far away as Glenwood Springs to attend the school and as more children rode the van, the idea of moving the school to a mid-valley location began to simmer. Board members continued to come from our founding families but they began to reach into the greater Waldorf community, visiting other schools, attending workshops, even speaking at Waldorf conferences. They also reached into the valley for possible locations for a new school but were turned back after each attempt.

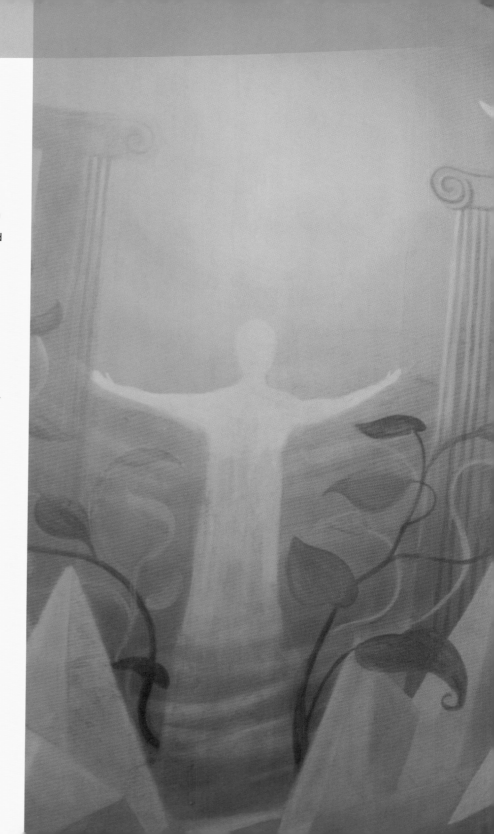

In 1995, our fifth year, Frances Lewis started a new first grade with seven children, which grew to twelve in a combined first/second the next year. The faculty struggled with the foreign language program; Spanish and German were offered, but only intermittently as teachers came and left. Betsy, assisted by Kate Friesen, continued with highly artistic handwork and calligraphy. Patty Fox, Patty Doyle and Frances offered drawing, beeswax modeling and painting. Mr. Moore wowed us with speech, drama and eurythmy lessons and performances that were the pinnacle of each year. His program, as well as the orchestra and choir, were boosted by Valerie Lee, who joined us as eurythmy accompanist and then music teacher.

In mid-winter, Patty Doyle announced her engagement to Adam Stopeck. They planned a July wedding followed by a move to Sacramento where Adam, inspired by Patty and René Querido, would begin his Waldorf training. Despite our own struggles, we had now inspired Adam, Kate Moga, Holly Richardson and Allison Kay to begin their Waldorf training, a sign of promise for the future. When we interviewed Cathy Fisher to open a mid-valley Children's Garden in Blue Lake and Robin Marcus to replace Patty Doyle in the third/fourth grade – and discovered they were childhood friends – we felt the stars were aligned in our favor.

As indeed they were. For in the fall of 1996, Felicia Winograd, one of our dedicated parents, found our new home: a thirteen-acre homestead on the river between Basalt and Carbondale, twenty-five miles from Aspen.

Steven Moore's antics have fifth graders bowing down! 1995

The early childhood of our school was past, and with it the tenderness of those years. By the end of summer, 1997, we had replaced the cells of our first body in Aspen with a spectacular new one in Carbondale. The major organs of board and faculty with some committees and task forces were maturing, but new organs were awaiting recognition. The parent council was especially anxious though we didn't know it yet.

During the second seven-year cycle, seven to fourteen, the child travels into new territory in which true emotions are experienced and tested.

While some of the journey to a healthy feeling life is along a scenic route, there are bumps, potholes and blind curves, especially during the nine- and twelve-year change, when the road can become challenging. The force of mature thinking, the ego, which will begin to take full control during the late teenage years, is an inattentive passenger at seven and begins driver's training only at twelve to fourteen. Years of practice are needed to avoid the hazards brought on by undisciplined emotions. We were in for a wild ride.

Frances Lewis

Being a Waldorf teacher is a journey of self discovery, re-education, sacrifice and dedication.

I always loved children and felt teaching was my calling. But I wanted to educate differently, to nurture the soul as well as teach academics. In the spring of 1996, Betsy Engelman brought the Waldorf students' art and handwork into the Valley Kids Show at the Aspen Art Museum where I was working. It was beautiful and distinctively different from everything else. After many conversations with the development director there, Kathryn King, she approached me to start the new first grade and it seemed my destiny was coming to meet me. But after the first year, I was convinced I couldn't hold a class. The children ran away from me, out the door and down the block. All they wanted was to be back in the kindergarten with Mrs. Kanipe. I thought I wasn't meant to be a teacher but I couldn't give the class over to someone else in that ragged condition so I had to teach just one more year.

That summer I took Jack Petrash's course on teaching through the grades at the Waldorf Institute in Waterville, Maine and saw a practical side to the education that made a lot of sense. I met Julianna Lichatz, who now teaches here, and was relieved to find a Waldorf person full of enthusiasm and youthful energy with pink cheeks because up until then, the adults I'd met at conferences were grey-faced intellectuals. I wondered, "If we're supposed to teach so that people are rosy pink, why is everyone so grey?"

I was leery of the spiritual side of anthroposophy, too, and had the question, "Am I involved in a cult?"

Jack inspired me and my second year was so much better with a combined class of twelve that I thought, "Maybe I am meant to do this." On Christmas Eve I called Eugene Schwartz to ask if I could still enroll in the teacher training course he'd started in the summer and he said yes, if I could be in New York by January 1st! I scrambled, enrolled in the course and returned to Sunbridge College for two weeks in winter and a month in summer for three years. I felt a real connection with Eugene and his style of Waldorf teaching. Still, every year I thought, "I'll stay just one more year." It wasn't until I was teaching a combined fourth/fifth grade that I decided I'd see it through to eighth grade – and then only because it was a year of crisis and Patty Fox told me if I didn't stay with it, I wouldn't survive a marriage either!

Ms Lewis' class participates with students from five regional Waldorf schools in the Greek pentathalon.

Being a Waldorf teacher is a journey of self-discovery, re-education, sacrifice and dedication. It was a challenge to make the curriculum fit a combined group but I was young and naïve and found I had a pioneering spirit and the flexibility I needed. When we moved to the new campus and my class grew to twenty-two, I found teaching a large class three times more fun than teaching seven. It was a trial by fire but I taught on the wings of grace. The parents saw something in me that they could support wholeheartedly and they gave me the gift of being their children's teacher.

When the faculty crisis came in January of 1999, it felt like being swept into the center of an intense fever. Students and faculty left or were in such pain that they weren't really present. By the end of the year, there were only four of us carrying the school and I thought it would fold. Still, I was committed to seeing it through and felt I owed it to the children to find a new sixth/seventh grade teacher to replace Robin Marcus. I went to Europe to get my dear friend Holly McSwain (now Richardson) who was completing her teacher training there thinking if I could have just one friend, one colleague that I really knew, maybe we could make it.

Holly came, and then Bill Fordham. I was excited because I was starving for depth and Bill was a mentor who had been involved in the education for a long time. That year, teaching fifth/sixth grade, I could feel a pull between the older and younger students and I began developing the idea of split blocks for the upper grades. The board resisted because there was an economic advantage to keeping the class together, but the health of the class prevailed and at the end of the year I created a three-year block plan to finish the curriculum with both classes. Holly graduated her eighth grade and came back to share the teaching. When Holly left to nurture her pregnancy, Lyman Jackson came with his big booming voice and plans to build a mechanical car engine out of wood. The class loved him and I sensed that he was meant to be their future teacher. In June, I passed the baton and graduated myself along with the students who had formed my original first grade.

Ms Lewis and our dear Mr. Moore

I still find places in anthroposophy that make my stomach churn but it is deeply satisfying to work with adults who are trying to bring something meaningful into the world, and who embrace the concept that there is a spiritual world with which we are working. I learned that children do not come to us as blank slates but bring something substantive for use in their life journeys. The teacher has something of Truth with which to work. Teaching is an art of give and take, attentive meditation, observation and conscious action.

"It was a trial by fire but I taught on the wings of grace."

Nance Aldrich

Nance's son, Ben Snow, joined Frances' first class.

From the moment I walked into the White Mountain Waldorf preschool in Conway, New Hampshire, I knew Waldorf education was the path that would serve Ben Snow best. Without being aware of it, I was already raising him as a Waldorf child: no TV, wooden toys, calm, nurturing surroundings. In our homes we all have values that we want to teach our children. To have them constantly challenged is frustrating and difficult: "Should we say a grace?" "No one else does, Mom." You begin to think maybe it's not that important. But Waldorf supported our values and made them stronger. If you have that core, your tribe, you can go out into the world and fight the good fight.

When Ben Snow was four, we were living near my folks in New Hampshire and their church had a small preschool where I took Ben to observe. There were garish plastic toys, mostly broken. The children were scribbling on dittos; a video was playing loudly. It was total sensory overload and it bred chaos. I was heartbroken that I was faced with leaving my child in such surroundings. I left crying and unsettled but instinct told me there had to be another option. Looking for a place to turn around, I passed a neat white fence surrounding a cottage with flowers in the yard and a little sign: White Mountain Waldorf School. I had a friend whose child loved her Waldorf preschool so I parked, wiped my eyes, and knocked. A dear woman opened the door, extended her hand and invited us to join the class for story. It was love at first sight. There were the same wooden toys I'd chosen for Ben Snow at home, soft colors, cheerful voices, happy, focused children. We'd come home!

When my husband Jef was interviewed for the job of ski patrol director at Aspen Mountain, I sent him off saying, "Only if there's a Waldorf school!" Not only did he return with news of the growing Aspen Waldorf School but also, my old friend Barbi Sheffer, with whom I'd taught skiing at Keystone, had her daughter, Brooke, in the first grade. Barbi and I had connected in Keystone but once you share Waldorf, your souls are connected.

Ben Snow had trouble learning to read and it became apparent that he was severely dyslexic. He could have been tested, perhaps he should have been, but I didn't want him labeled and I was afraid that ADHD would also be a factor and drugs would be recommended. But Frannie, Miss Lewis, had faith in him so I had faith in him too. It's part of the beauty of having the same teacher all eight years. She knew Ben Snow better than anyone. Having not been labeled, I now feel that my son has turned out exactly the way he's supposed to be.

"If you have that core, your tribe, you can go out into the world and fight the good fight."

We left the valley to enroll Ben Snow in a Waldorf high school but our first attempt failed, so he repeated eighth grade in a public school. There he was taught using the Orton-Gillingham method and he's learned to read more fluently. He was on the honor roll, very outspoken and verbal, a leader. "He thinks!" the teachers said. "He has ideas! He loves to learn!" But he begged to return to Waldorf. He's such a heart child, the aesthetic qualities of his surroundings are as important to him as spirited teachers, and the soulless buildings hurt him as much as the mediocre curriculum. We moved again so that he could attend High Mowing Waldorf High School. Immediately he was singing on his way to school and when I asked if he liked his classmates he replied, "They're Waldorf kids, Mom. They just accept you for who you are."

The most beautiful thing happened when Ben Snow was in eighth grade at the Waldorf School on the Roaring Fork. Every year the class performs a play and Ben Snow was always given small parts because

Ben Snow

it was so hard for him to learn his lines. In first grade he was a lion and stood frozen on the stage, eyes bugged out. By eighth grade, it was becoming painfully obvious that he wasn't keeping up with his class-mates academically and he needed to shine somewhere. The play was *Much Ado About Nothing* and Ben Snow intimated to me that he would love the challenge of playing Benedict, one of the leading roles. I spoke with Mr. Moore, the director, and despite his strong reservations, he agreed to give Ben the part. After reading how dyslexic actor Tom Cruise learns all his lines by listen-ing to them on tape, Mr. Moore did the same for Ben, a feat in itself from a devoted teacher. Well, Ben Snow nailed it! He shined like a bright star and I was in awe.

Fourth grade class trip to Mesa Verde

Drama: Why is *"the play the thing"*?

While we may think of theater as "entertainment," we find ourselves deeply touched by a play when complex characters are embodied by penetrating artists. Since ancient Greece, drama has held the potential for cathartic, even life-changing effect. Willingly or not, as in the case of Hamlet's Claudius, humans cannot but be affected when a committed actor gives life to a dramatic character. We live the comedy and tragedy as well. (This is, in fact, a key to the art of Waldorf education. The best teachers are those who live deeply into the stories they tell, the lessons they create. Like the theater audience, their heroic, tragic and comic characters become a daily addition to their students' individuality.) If empathy with the character on the stage is possible for the audience, how much more so for the actor, child or adult?

In Waldorf schools, every class presents a play every year and every child has a part. All year, speech exercises are a conscious part of the main lesson. Movement and gesture are practiced in eurythmy class and morning circle. Teachers choose a play or write an original one suited to the class, a play that will move the children through an enlivening, nurturing or empowering experience. As the play approaches, parts are chosen. Disappointments, fears and over-exuberance must be dealt with; lines must be memorized. Costume and stage design involve the parent community. In the first grade, the plays are simple fairy tales comprised largely of choral speaking. Year by year the plays become more complex, reflecting a curriculum which in turn reflects the development of human consciousness. By eighth grade, a full scale Shakespearean production is possible.

*Ayla Wayman and Taylor Luck in **Lancelot and Guinevere***

60

How does the drama curriculum affect the student? On a practical level, while many adults are hesitant if not terrified to stand before an audience, Waldorf students rarely are. They have practiced projection, clarity and dramatic emphasis for eight years and can be understood and heard without amplification. Their gestures are sincere, augmenting their messages in conversations with friends as well as in public speaking. On a social level, younger students have seen their teachers and parents come together to create something new in the world. As they've grown older, they've worked with costume and stage design, lighting and props and found strengths and weaknesses in their peers that must be accommodated. Inwardly, their development has been immeasurably enhanced by

Nathan Ulrich, Max Ramge, Paul Struempler and Kidd Martin Baran in **Lancelot and Guinevere**

having "tried on" different characters during their formative years. When students have the opportunity to learn who they are and who they are not on stage, they are unlikely to imitate unsavory characters in life. They'll emulate the heroes and heroines who serve humanity, for they have embodied those characters and found their secrets to happiness.

Maureen Fox, Alison Biehert, Tyler Henderson, Alicia Parker and Tae Westcott in Chaucer's **Canterbury Tales**

Barbara Allen

Barbara, our "fairy godmother," worked behind the scenes making treats for board meetings, handwork creations for festivals and "world-famous" waffles for the kindergarteners.

My interest in Waldorf education began with Patty Fox's Colorado Mountain College class. I was floundering, looking for something meaningful to do with the rest of my life. There was something about my early fifties…I had this energy. And I had a grandson who was baffling to me. The CMC class was so rich with beauty, song, handwork and puppetry – it was quite an impulse, really. I think I was in need of something spiritual too, and anthroposophy, combined with finding people I'd known in Denver theater years before – Steven Moore and Merlyn Querido – captured me. It changed me. Now I feel that it so permeates my life I don't even think about it.

I was on the fringe, not a parent, but I wanted to do something useful and attended the workshops. I asked Patty, "What can I do?" and she said, "You can be on the board," and so I started pitching in, helping with festivals, making puppets, balancing the books. The third year, when CP Kanipe went to California for a week of training, I assisted Jo Richter in the kindergarten. The next year I was CP's assistant. I transformed a black room in the Yellow Brick that had been used for theater into a "peach blossom" kindergarten that summer and I loved being there. I assisted for two years, but especially loved the puppetry and the handwork that went into them. I later attended several workshops and have written and performed puppet plays locally.

I loved the children but by the sixth year of the school, I chose to work in the office and continued there until the school moved to Carbondale at the end of the year. I did do some lazuring for the new building but found I couldn't manage the drive. When Cathy Fisher came back to Aspen in 1998, I assisted her and we had a very special relationship. We still do.

I felt at times I wasn't appreciated. I think we all did. It took me some time to realize, it's not about me. There was something bigger. I'm really happy now to have been part of the wonderfully warm early years of the school. If I were to identify one challenge for the future, it would be some form of community housing to settle the people working at the school. It was talked about at one time and I can still envision a larger community there.

Bil Dunaway, owner of "The Aspen Times" assured that our initiative was well-covered in the Times and with his wife, Barbara Allen, arranged a low-interest loan to finance the purchase of the Carbondale property.

"I can envision a larger community."

Robin Marcus Grey

Robin took over Patty Doyle's class in third grade, the first class to journey from kindergarten to graduation.

Home in Birmingham, Alabama after college and a year in the West, I met Sheila Rubin who had a small Waldorf kindergarten. As unfamiliar as it was, it was totally familiar. I began assisting Sheila and one day I came upon a brochure from the Rudolf Steiner Institute, an anthroposophic summer camp for adults in Waterville, Maine. I was so taken by the brochure that I enrolled. I met amazing people my own age as well as older "Anthropops" who led and inspired us newcomers. I took a biography class with an Englishwoman, Margly Matthews who introduced me to Suzanne Downs, puppeteer and instant friend. They told me that my next step was to go to Emerson and enroll in teacher training. I went home and within three weeks my ever-supportive mom made it happen, a year in England.

My foundation year was one of the most awakening experiences of my life. It answered the spiritual and emotional questions my soul had been yearning to ask. I was so open,

so excited and so connected to my "golden circle" of fellow students from twenty-eight countries. We had our seventh year reunion at Emerson in July of 2002 and it was interesting to learn that my story is not an anomaly. Only three of the thirty-five are still teaching.

After completing my training at Sunbridge College in Spring Valley, New York, I knew that I wanted to be in Colorado, so Eugene Schwartz arranged for me to student-teach at the Shepherd Valley Waldorf School in Boulder. I hoped to take a first grade class there but came to Aspen for an interview. The school was still in its "family" stage of development, and that meant that the parents, board and faculty all wanted to have a role in the interview process, though I had been taught that the faculty was solely responsible for hiring. I called Eugene to ask his advice and he said this was an example of "trial by fire," a phenomenon that new teachers often encounter, and told me to refuse the mass interview.

It was a dreary, rainy day back in Spring Valley when Aspen called to offer me the job. I walked outside for fresh air and suddenly there appeared a double rainbow! I thought, "I guess I'm going to Aspen." It was the first of many double rainbows.

I loved my bright yellow room and my sweet class of third and fourth graders, but I felt intimidated by the ghost of Patty Doyle, their much-loved first teacher. Nonetheless I felt deeply connected to the children and the teachers. I found my strengths were creating form, structure and a sense of community within the class, promoting respect and nurturing the human being.

Brittany Fortier, Brooke Sheffer and Megan Schlussler with their knitted puppets

The highlight of the year was our play, *Joseph and His Coat of Many Colors*, which the children spoke strongly and confidently in the cavernous gym.

Early that year, we found the new land in Carbondale and built the straw-bale school that summer. The raising of the bales was incredible and I personally loved the lazuring, but felt obligated to work all the time. New children joined my class that fall and there were many adult efforts to incorporate new families, new policies and new committees that I felt had more in common with public schools than Waldorf schools. This absorbed as much time as teaching.

As a young school trying to fill the new classrooms that we had built, we accepted virtually every applicant. New families entered my class so quickly that there was no time for them to study, no less understand, all of the qualities and methods that made our Waldorf setting so different from other schools. Some families could not wait for our curriculum and methods to show the positive results they almost always do show, in time. Several special-needs children came and left my class within months. Their disappointed parents, not having been cautioned that Waldorf education requires patience and perseverance, criticized my teaching or the school's "lack of accountability."

I was caught off-guard by the passions that a misunderstanding of Waldorf education can arouse. The volatile atmosphere that built up around these issues made it hard for me to appear in school every day, but the moment I saw the children I stood tall and focused. The children never experienced my inner turmoil; they always received the best that I had to give.

The life of a Waldorf school is so rich and multilayered that I could receive nurturance from our Winterfaire, from the faculty eurythmy that Steven Moore led, and from his solo rendition of *O Holy Night*. His performance stood as a moment of spiritual serenity in the midst of my struggles with parents and colleagues. But the pressures and misunderstandings that can arise all too readily in a young school led by an inexperienced faculty overshadowed the joys of the classroom and the winter festivals; I felt that I had no choice but to leave.

In spite of my deep sorrow at having to take this step, I am glad that it was Holly McSwain (Richardson) who came to take my class, and perhaps that was destiny, too. I am grateful to say that I have life-long relationships with many of my former students. I hope that my experiences, however painful or unfounded they might have been, have in some way helped the school become wiser and more consequential about its growth and colleagueship.

"The lasting gift of my work at the school is my significant, life long relationships."

Cathy Fisher

Ms Cathy almost single-handedly created the new Blue Lake kindergarten before her first day of teaching.

I always knew I wanted to work with children, but the small college I attended didn't have an education department so I majored in psychology. After college, I researched many educational philosophies but couldn't find what I wanted and spent a winter serving lattes and snowboarding in Bend, Oregon. There I met Waldorf education, at an après-ski restaurant, when I sat next to a Waldorf kindergarten teacher! With every word out of her mouth, I got more excited. This was what I had been searching for! I observed her kindergarten and found it magical, all that I believed in but didn't yet know. The next fall, I moved to Eugene and entered the two-year training.

Rudolf Steiner's insightful views on teaching the young child kept me motivated, but the foundation year studies threw me for a loop. I was open to learning about anthroposophy but it was not as transforming for me as it was for others in the class. Still, at the end of the two years, I felt the world was my oyster; I could go anywhere to teach in a Waldorf school. I already loved Boulder so I applied there and in Denver before I learned there was a school in Aspen. All I remember of my city interviews was lots of traffic. But at the end of the trip, I rented a car to drive to Aspen. As I drove up Hallam Street, I felt the same excitement I had felt when I met the woman in Bend, a sort of "coming home," that this had been waiting for me forever. Patty Fox and CP Kanipe were on the steps and there was a silent but instant, "Yes!" among us. I joined their faculty meeting and saw a name familiar from childhood on their agenda.

Cathy with Grace Schultz, 1997

"Could this Robin Marcus be from Birmingham, Alabama?" When they said yes, I was stunned. No one goes to Waldorf training from Birmingham, but here was a friend with whom I'd played softball in elementary school, another sign that everything was coming together.

However, I was being interviewed for a class that didn't exist and in retrospect, I was a crazy lady. I was to open a kindergarten in the mid-valley the next fall with no space, no students and no furniture, only my enthusiasm and commitment.

I researched spaces, met with city planners, shopped at thrift stores and by fall, I opened the Children's Garden in the Blue Lake Community Center. My first home interview was with Summer Cole and I felt so warmly received that I thought, "I can do this!" Still, I might not have been able to do it without Christy Braeger, who had been CP's assistant in Aspen. She had such a way with children, of greeting them coming down from the heavens, that I learned more from her than I did from my training.

And there was so much work with puppet plays, Mommy & Me, anything that would build interest. That summer it was exhilarating to have a hand in building the school and I felt that I'd started something new in the mid-valley. When the school opened, my kindergarten had fifteen children, a real class, and I was a real teacher blossoming in it. Sometime during that year, I happened to sit next to Barbara Allen during a workshop with Eugene Schwartz. She leaned toward me and whispered, "I have a fantasy about working with you in the kindergarten." I was puzzled, but at the end of the year Helena Hurrell, who had taken the kindergarten in Aspen, asked me to switch places with her. Her connections were downvalley and mine were in Aspen. So it came about that Barbara and I began working together in Aspen in 1998. We started with enrollment high, the parents and class euphoric. Barbara volunteered her time three days a week, a strong, loving presence in the kindergarten. It was the start of a beautiful friendship. Barbara's crafts for Mommy & Me were so inspired that people still come up to me to say, "I'm using my silk mobile now for my third baby!"

Despite the beauty of our little kindergarten, the growing pains of the Waldorf school in Carbondale made it difficult for the faculty to give equal attention to both the Aspen and the downvalley sites. Although we were connected by a common highway, Route 82, the heavy load of responsibilities shouldered by teachers and parents alike made communication challenging.

By the third year in Aspen, enrollment had dwindled to seven children. I knew I was going to have to let go but I wanted to make that last year special – and I did. We were a family of fun-loving brothers and sisters. It was the best year ever until asbestos was discovered in the Yellow Brick School. I took the children to my little cabin for two weeks until Jennifer Chandler, my after-care provider, connected us with the Silver Lining Ranch. We moved back into the Yellow Brick two long months later and only after washing and scrubbing every item, every knife, fork, spoon, thimble and toy in the whole room.

When I decided to resign after five years with the school, I couldn't help but be sad, but grateful for the thanks from my wonderful parents and children.

I know I grew through my experience at the Waldorf School on the Roaring Fork. I learned to find balance in my life, to make room for my marriage, for travel, and for other interests. The lasting gift of my work at the school is my significant, lifelong relationships.

Summer Cole

Summer opened the door for our transition to the mid-valley campus.

My first experience of Waldorf was at the Mayfaire in Aspen in 1993. We had just moved here; Matthew was three and home with me. The name "Waldorf" rang a bell because my parents were both teachers in Pasadena and my mom had a friend who took her daughter out of the academically-pushed school I attended and sent her to the Pasadena Waldorf School of which she spoke very highly. But my real introduction was a year later at a talk given in Basalt by Kim McCarty, a visiting Waldorf kindergarten teacher from Sacramento. I just "got it" that day. Patty told me later that she and Kim said afterwards, "That woman's going to be a Waldorf teacher someday." That hasn't happened – yet – but what I heard clicked because my education was so different, and always I'd been screaming to get out. It made such sense to me I knew I wanted this for my children.

The Waldorf school was in Aspen and we were in Basalt. We couldn't afford either the tuition or the drive, so I enrolled Matthew half days in the Basalt kindergarten even though he was a little young for his class. At the end of the year it was clear to us that he needed more time before going on to first grade. When Melinda Schultz told me about the Waldorf satellite kindergarten opening at Blue Lake, I enrolled both Matthew and Kenzie. It felt peaceful and right. The Children's Garden was very minimal in the way of toys and that particular space had to be set up and taken down each week, but Miss Cathy and Miss Christy transformed it. I'll never forget arriving one day with all of the children playing a made-up trading game with rocks. They were so busy, they didn't want to leave. And it was just rocks! What a sharp contrast

to the daycare upstairs filled with tons of bright-colored "stuff." Here, the children were truly happy and so creative with next to nothing. It amazed me because the pervasive message in our society is "our children need lots and lots of stuff to be content in their play time." I was drawn to the simplicity and rhythm. My children were deeply satisfied and so were we.

I prayed that the school would find the perfect land, and the summer after that year we helped build the first building at the new campus. I stacked straw bales and lazured with Charles Andrade and a group of moms. I was there as much as could be because I enjoyed painting and participating in this group endeavor. I served on the parent council in its infantile stage for three years as we were trying to form it, which was a lot of hard

"It's all been good."

work. But building community takes hard work, serving and giving of yourself. It's been the most fulfilling and best education for me and my children. In 2001, I had Hannah and backed off to care for my baby, but my husband, Chuck, took over for our family, first serving on the board and then as board president. Since then I've found myself involved in the adult choir, The Waldorf Revelers, which has brought richness and depth to my life, our lives. Matthew has graduated, Kenzie will graduate in 2007 and sweet Hannah will start her quest through the grades. It has truly been a great learning and growing experience for all of us. We feel so blessed.

Kate Friesen and Peter Westcott

Peter was a friendly presence in the public schools, Kate a knowing mother. They stood back but slowly were drawn into the Waldorf school with Peter working on the buildings and Kate teaching.

Peter: I have been teaching in the Aspen Middle School since 1987 and when Betsy Engelman and Patty Fox were hosting informative teas for the public school teachers, I went to several. I came home and said to Kate, "I think you should come to these meetings. I think you'd like what they do." From then on, I was a friendly face in the public schools, which, not surprisingly, did not embrace the idea of incorporating a Waldorf track. I must say, though, the public school staff is finally starting to notice how engaged our kids are in education. I recently heard the school secretary say, "Those kids from the Waldorf school are really different."

We were invited to be on the advisory board when the school opened but we stood back, looking but not jumping in. When Tae was ready to start first grade we decided to take the leap and applied for admission, but there was no first grade class for him. We reluctantly enrolled him in the Basalt schools from September to December, when we left the valley for a teacher exchange in Australia.

Kate: After Peter told me about the meetings, I enrolled in Patty Fox's Waldorf Ideas class in Carbondale and I enjoyed that. While in Australia, we visited several Waldorf schools and learned more about them. But when we returned from Australia, I was in such severe culture shock that I decided to home-school Tae the rest of the year, teaching him to knit and play recorder in addition to his other subjects. The next year we enrolled him in Patty's fourth grade even though he would be the only third grader and the only boy in the class. There were times when we felt the Waldorf curriculum was wasted on Tae, who wanted to be totally into the 21st century. But the small class of girls was nurturing and in high school he sought the same sort of nice, happy kids. Of course we panicked before he started there, but the transition was a non-issue.

We enrolled Claire in the kindergarten with CP and Barbara Allen. Then she started first grade with Frances Lewis. Frances was as new to Waldorf as the kindergartners were to first grade. But that was the last year we worried. By the next year, Frances had a class of happy children and the curriculum was a perfect fit for Frances and her class.

Peter: In the public school, we change the curriculum all the time, but there doesn't seem to be any real reason behind the changes other than, perhaps, aligning it with the Colorado State Assessment Program. The thing I love about Waldorf is that there's a reason behind every aspect of the curriculum at every level – and a reason behind the reason behind the reason.

Kate: I remember once when Patty Fox related to me how, working with the curriculum content and its purpose, she felt her own consciousness evolve in a way that mirrored the evolution of human consciousness she was teaching. She was referring to how humans have developed higher perceptions as they have evolved and how the growing child (and his teacher!) goes through the same changes. Although I nodded, and celebrated with her, I didn't understand what she was talking about. But now, after working with the genius of the curriculum more deeply, I get the same kind of "aha" moments all the time.

Peter: Kate immediately began to volunteer, driving the bus and helping with handwork. I thought I was going to escape volunteering but then the building began. I was in charge of organizing the straw-bale volunteers for the first building while Kate provided care for the children of the volunteers at our home. We became full-time volunteers. I remember being hot and sticky from the straw, frustrated by the demands of my full-time volunteer job, and sneaking out to the sluice box beyond the second pond to skinny dip. I worked on the kindergarten building, too, and helped with class trips several times, especially canoeing in Lake Powell.

Kate: By 1996, I was so involved in the handwork that I decided to enroll in the applied arts training in Sunbridge College, which included the wood and clay curriculum. I worked with Betsy Engelman and later with Lisa Huber, Jill Scher and David Franklin coordinating the applied arts curriculum. Early in 2001, I taught a physics block for Frances and just loved it. When the combined fourth/fifth grade class

needed a teacher, I agreed first to take a couple of blocks, then a few more. Eventually, the school was able to split Ms Lewis' class and I became a full time teacher. Lyman Jackson took the eighth grade through graduation in 2005 and I will graduate my class in June 2006.

Peter: One evening not long after we joined the school, there came a knock on the door and in walked CP and Stephen Kanipe and Kathryn King with Pam Doble wearing a wreath of candles, singing. It was December 13th, Santa Lucia Day, a Swedish tradition in which the oldest girl, wearing a crown of candles, brings holiday songs and treats to her family. Kate was spinning. Tae and Claire were playing with their wooden blocks on the floor. I was sitting by the fire, reading. They thought we were the perfect Waldorf family! They didn't know that moments before, the scene had been a bit chaotic. But our Santa Lucia visit was magical, and really, I think Waldorf has been perfect for us.

Science in the Waldorf School

By Kate Friesen

The study of science in the Waldorf school begins in the pre-school years. The abundant hours that the youngest members of our school spend outdoors nurture a life-long study of nature built on observation and imagination. In these hours the children develop as much "oneness" with nature as is possible given our culture's indoor orientation. They learn about shade and sun, wet and dry, enclosed and open, and the life forms that inhabit these polarities. Each child has intimate experiences with bugs, the downward trickle of a stream, the expansive feeling of standing on top of the hill and the safe enclosure provided by giant lilac bushes. Through nature stories begun in kindergarten and continued in the early grades – tales of the gnome's secrets and the fairy's reverence for living things – imaginations develop a deep connection with all life. This connection serves the children in later years when their knowledge is deepened by natural history. The celebration of seasonal festivals furthers this healthy feeling relationship that young children must have in order to become stewards of the environment in later years.

In fourth grade, the study of animals requires sharper observation as children learn how an animal's form reflects its function as well as its character. After observing these relationships in many animals, children see similar abilities and characteristics in themselves and they discover that part of being human is being aware of these qualities and keeping them in balance. The study of plants opens a new kingdom to the observant fifth grader. Again the form, function and characteristics of different plants, from simple to complex, awaken the children's ability to observe. Plants are studied in the context of their relationship to their environment, the soil and the climate. Contrasting the

Claire Westcott, Katelyn Woolcott and Frances Lewis

stems with the roots, the flowers with the leaves, or even the characteristics of moss with those of the oak helps develop the children's ability to think about their observations. The mineral kingdom is studied in sixth grade by looking at the whole earth, its mountains, rivers and changing forms, and then its minerals.

Physics is introduced through fun, active experiments. The properties of sound, light, heat and magnetism are experienced and observed through simple, clear experiments chosen to sharpen the students' observation skills. Subjective as well as objective observations are encouraged because feelings about phenomena connect the physical world to our personal experience. Comparison of subjective observations also points out the need for objectivity when, in seventh grade, objective measurement of experimental results in physics is introduced.

The laws of polarity and transformation are the underpinnings of seventh grade science. The life sciences are extended to a study of health and nutrition in which students learn both how the body functions and the responsibility we each have to care for our bodies. The mechanics of simple machines brings an understanding of how the tools that humans have created work to help us. The relationship between magnets and electricity is observed. The laws of chemical combustion are experienced with great interest! Again, polarity and transformation are observed in smoke and ash, in acids and bases, and even within each person's feeling life. When children experience the transformation of matter, the possibility of inner transformation becomes real.

The eighth grader is ready to deepen the experiences of previous years. In life science, students study the anatomy of the skeletal and muscular systems, the eye and ear. In physics, properties of light, heat and sound are extended as we ask students to look beyond the classroom into the real world. We ask not only what, but when and where in the world a phenomenon happens, why it happens and who discovered it and applied it to new uses. Electromagnetism is explored and time is spent on hydraulics and aeromechanics, which helps build a conceptual framework for a block devoted to meteorology. In chemistry, again through exciting demonstrations and experiments, students study sugars, carbohydrates, fat and oils, proteins and even cosmetics. What we eat comes alive on a brand new level of understanding. In the eighth grade year, the students face the world directly.

Science in the Waldorf school strives to cultivate our students' sense of wonder. We want to stimulate their curiosity and sharpen their observational skills so that they develop a lively and imaginative interest in the world around them. By emphasizing observation, we help children draw conclusions, make judgments and develop concepts so that they will apply their knowledge in meaningful and responsible ways when they enter the world as adults.

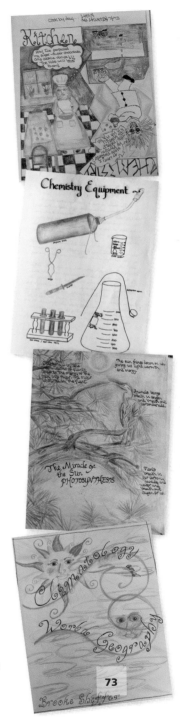

73

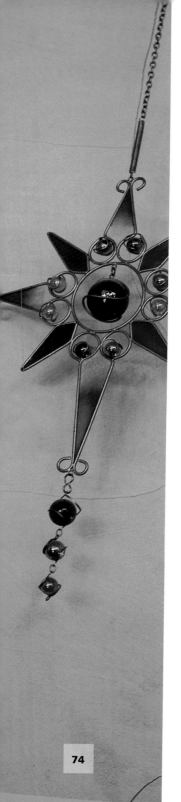

Felicia Winograd

Felicia, a Waldorf graduate from Germany, enrolled her son, lent her expertise – and found our new home.

I was born in Aachen, Germany in 1960. My parents were Holocaust survivors and moved to Israel when I was six months old. We moved back to Germany in 1966, before the Seven-Day War. I was enrolled in the public school but spoke German poorly with a Hebrew accent. This provoked my classmates and my mom soon found the 800-student Munich Waldorf School, the only really safe school for Jewish kids at that time.

It's interesting to compare the European curriculum to ours. We went to school from 8:00 to 1:30 with short breaks and then came home for lunch and about six hours of homework. We often had school on Saturday. We studied English and French from first grade on, Ancient Greek in seventh grade and Latin from eighth grade through high school. That's been my vision for our Waldorf school and I've lobbied to achieve it. I especially remember the gardening because our school was in central Munich and we went to the Friedel-Eder Schule on the outskirts of the city for gardening classes. This was a special Waldorf school for Downs syndrome children. We were assigned a partner and worked together in the garden. It was a wonderful experience and took away the fear of "different."

There were at least forty kids in my class, a lot for one teacher. We had a mix of teachers from those who turned me off to anthroposophy to the young, unstarched types. Many kids who had been expelled from public schools came to our school and there were several tragedies. I think this mix, and the experiences we went through together, gave all of us great confidence and made us appreciate what we had. Most of us graduated from the Waldorf school with a strong sense of what is to come and very little fear of life. I can't understand it when a young person says, "I couldn't travel there. I don't speak the language."

I married Eric in Aspen in 1988. We traveled around the world and Josh was born in 1990. When we returned to Aspen I learned there was a new Waldorf school and said, "Oh! That's where he will go to school." He began kindergarten in 1992 and joined Frances Lewis' class in 1996. He stayed ten years, for as long as Frances was his teacher.

I taught German for a while but was building a house, starting a floral design business, working on the board of trustees and being a mother. We were actively looking for land at that time and I told my friend, Gabriella Sutro, a realtor in Carbondale, that she had to help us. We had a long list of requirements: trees, water, non-toxic soil, accessibility, suitable zoning and so on. On September 23, 1996, Gabriella called to tell me that a property two miles from my house had come onto the market. We met there and I knew instantly, this was it. I called the teachers and board members who walked the land that afternoon and they knew, too.

Intense retreats and board meetings followed. We hired Jeff Dickinson as our architect and the questions began: "What do you want? Be specific. Envision. Write it down." The wheels turned too slowly for my intensity, but it's an amazing school.

I was troubled by the number of teachers who came and went, but was equally amazed at the resourcefulness of our community. Sometimes I thought we worked better when oil was poured on the fire. I guess these are the struggles of youth and I am so grateful there was a Waldorf school for Josh even if it meant trial and error. There could be no other choice for me.

"Most of us graduated from the Waldorf school with a strong sense of what is to come and very little fear of life."

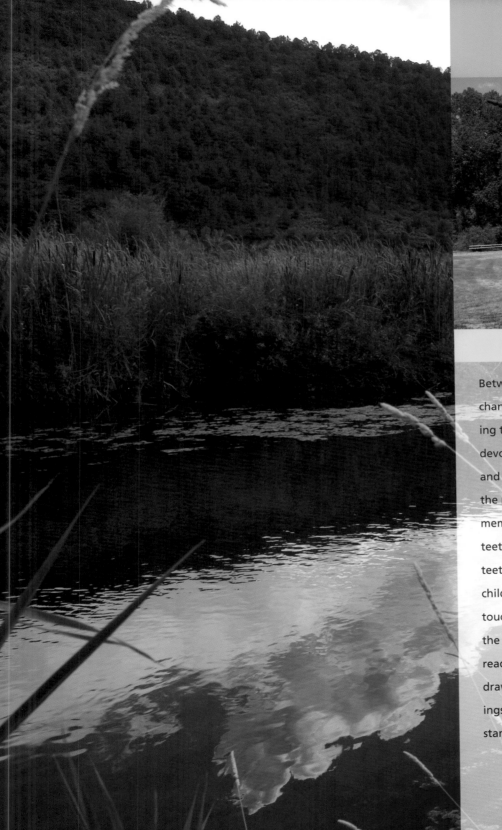

Chapter 4

Building the New Body

Between five and seven, physical changes occur in children indicating that the energy that has been devoted to the growth of skeleton and muscles, and differentiation of the metabolic organs, is available for memory and learning. The soft milk teeth are replaced by the hard adult teeth. The limbs extend so that the child can reach over her head and touch the opposite ear. The arch of the foot becomes defined. School readiness is expressed in the child's drawings, too. In archetypal drawings of person-house-tree, the person stands firmly on the earth with hands and feet, fingers and toes, eyes and mouth as if saying, "I'm here! I'm ready to begin!" The house has a door into the awakening mind and, self-aware, a window to look out of. There may be a chimney and smoke, indications that there's already independent thinking going on. The tree stands straight and tall with limbs reaching into the world. All of this is an expression that the child now inhabits a new body. The seven-year cycle in which the human body replaces all of its old cells with new ones is complete.

The Land

Our precious school was at this juncture on September 23, 1996, when parent and board member Felicia Winograd called excitedly to tell us a piece of land that had been under contract just hours before had come back onto the market. We must come to Carbondale immediately to see it. Those who walked the land that late fall day were stunned at its perfection: an old homestead with bearing fruit trees, wetlands bordering the Roaring Fork River, a concrete barn that would serve for storage, and clear pasture land for a building site and play yard.

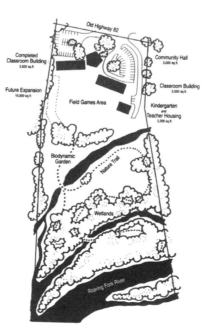

Within two days, Barbara Allen and Bil Dunaway and Barbi and Doug Sheffer had underwritten a purchase agreement. Our design team was already in place. Jeff Dickinson of Energy & Sustainable Design, who had attended an anthroposophic architecture workshop that summer, was open to combining Steiner's ideas with his green building designs. Stephen Kanipe, our board president and the chief building official for Aspen and Pitkin County, had just upgraded local building codes to incorporate straw-bale and other alternative building methods. Laura Bartels-Struempler, a friend of the Dickinsons, was building the first straw-bale home in the valley. Recognizing the time and money constraints of the project, Bill Engelman offered his best foreman, Matt Flink, to manage and streamline the construction process. Bob Schultz and Kathryn King brought them all together. The concepts of ecologically friendly straw-bale built by a volunteer community in a Steiner design formed the new body that our school would inhabit on its sixth birthday.

The West Wing

Built April to September, 1997

The board of trustees began meeting regularly at the Children's Garden in Blue Lake in order to move the consciousness to the mid-valley. A building committee formed. At Bob Schultz and Stephen Kanipe's suggestion, they hired David Michaelson and Tim Malloy to shepherd the purchase through a land use permit, for when we'd closed on the land, the only permitted uses were residential – and a release valve for the valley's main gas line! We breathed a huge sigh when Tim announced that in the first of a long series of approvals, the conditional use – school – had also been approved!

While the long road to a building permit was being walked by the board and building committee, the faculty was talking to Jeff about classroom size and administrative needs and to Kathryn about color and shape. During the winter the footprint for the campus build-out was drawn up and the building permits approved.

Although the plans went steadily forward, not everyone could imagine that we could finance even the first building. Mark Finser and Ann Stahl from the Rudolf Steiner Foundation came for a week, meeting individually with every faculty and board member and every parent to help us answer the questions, "Is there enough support? Can we afford this?" After the week they gave us a resounding "Yes!" and helped us design a pledge community to which all of our families subscribed at whatever level they could afford. By spring, the first building of five classrooms, two bathrooms and an office – later to be used as the school library – was designed, approved and financed.

With golden spades painted by Doug Sheffer and songs led by Valerie Lee, the children broke ground for the new building on April 12, 1997. Stephen Kanipe's speech at the ground-breaking included Goethe's quote on dreams, commitment and boldness, and concluded with the proclamation, "And now, may all who know this place, know it as the WALDORF SCHOOL ON THE ROARING FORK!" Constructing the first building became the greater process of building a community that included everyone in the school and extended into the wider community. The west wing was built in eighteen weeks and four days because our business partners, including Valley Lumber, Grand Junction Pipe, Mountain Blue Turf Farm and many others, went beyond the call. After six years of festivals, events, workshops and rent payments at our Aspen location we finally had the beginning of our own campus. Up to this point the foundation of the school was built on the investment of time and money by our founders. Now, we had to reach out to a larger community.

The East Wing, first addition

Built June to September, 1998

The prospect of another building the next year was overwhelming, and so the interim plan called for combining a new first grade with the existing one, giving us a year to recover from the first round of construction. The school had been trying to avoid combinations for several years, but low enrollment in Aspen had made combined classes a necessity. Now, with enrollment nearly doubling, from forty-four to eighty-four children, new parents were determined to have a new building to house uncombined classes and promised to fund it.

Laura Bartels-Struempler agreed to be the construction boss and Patty Fox would attempt to gather volunteers from the exhausted community. Permits were issued and the building, two rooms of a planned five-classroom east wing, was begun in late spring and finished in September. The seventh/eighth grade, now grown to nineteen students, spent the first two weeks of the school year building a fence along the east boundary and meeting for classes on the benches south of the playground. When finishing touches were added, the combined lead class moved into the west room while music and eurythmy occupied the east room. A removable wall separated the two and provided desperately needed space for class plays, eurythmy performances, assemblies, community meetings and festivals. The whole school celebrated the addition, which was lazured by Charles Andrade and parents in a lovely rainbow of color.

East Wing

Early Childhood Center

The Early Childhood Center

April to September, 2000

The kindergarten building was carefully, meticulously thought through. Led by architect Jeff Dickinson, the building committee visited many Waldorf schools, gleaning design elements and incorporating them into straw-bale forms. The kindergarten teachers added inspired details. The building rose from the ground like a hobbit home, soft, round and inviting. New, ecologically sound materials were found for flooring, light fixtures and ceiling finishes. Large closets and miniature sinks matched perfectly the needs of early childhood. Although much of the building was contracted through construction manager Mark Wolfe, volunteers raised the bales, applied stucco and wall finishes, and landscaped.

Now the kindergartens could have a space of their own and the school could add another first grade. Meanwhile the blossoming interest in performing arts resulted in overflow crowds attending the Steven Moore directed plays making it apparent we needed a larger performance hall. The construction of such a hall would have to wait until the community could recharge its batteries after multiple building projects and the nine year change.

Stephen Kanipe

As the second board president, Stephen led us into our new body.

I was the board president when we found the land and was completely involved in the approval process, planning and building. We held group planning sessions almost every Saturday from November until the building was finished in September. Planners, attorneys, board members, teachers and parents gathered in our kindergarten in Blue Lake – everyone was welcome – to plan the next step forward. We held a contest to name the school. There were dozens of offerings and we spent several weeks trying them out: El Jebel Waldorf School, Aspen Valley Waldorf School, Elk Mountain Waldorf School, The Waldorf School on the Gas Valve Parcel...

"We started out and just kept going."

Then Steven Moore said, "Let's see how they look in eurythmy." When he came to the Waldorf School on the Roaring Fork, moved it and spoke it, it was terrific and we all knew it was the right name.

I remember so clearly the bale raising. The bales of straw came on a huge semi from the San Luis Valley. We arrived on the site and began with stretching exercises before raising the bales, but the concrete accomplishments of bale raising, wiring, lathe and plaster were not "the raising." What we "raised" was a community! It would never have happened with a construction crew. There were forces working far beyond the site itself. On the final exterior stucco day, when the color coat was being laid on, Jeff Dickinson stepped back and said, "It needs something else." He picked up a trowel and began dancing around the building, skip troweling as he danced. We followed behind him doing the same. What joy!

Doug Sheffer, Eric Altenbernd and Stephen Kanipe

My last meetings were at the beginning of the turmoil of 1998–'99. I knew land use. I knew planning and construction. I didn't know how to deal with confrontations and I slipped out. It was several years later that Valerie Lee asked me to join the adult choir and I slipped back in, but now I was a parent instead of an involved parent.

Kathryn King

Kathryn was the development coordinator during
the transition to the new school.

Waldorf education often attracts a group of highly educated parents who lead extremely full lives but are seeking some sort of balance. This was the case in the Roaring Fork Valley. I came to Aspen in late March of 1994 for a reunion of college friends and heard right away about a Waldorf school that was struggling with low enrollment and a defunct charter school proposal. Patty Fox was chairing meetings and she invited me to meet their group. By August, I was offered a job and a place to live. The Fortiers had just finished their new house, complete with a caretaker apartment into which I moved even before the family. The job of community development coordinator was fashioned and so I began a four-year journey with the school.

We were in the Yellow Brick School and Barbara Allen was in the office with me. The school in those days was in its earliest stages of accounting with a hand ledger method for keeping the books. Eventually, a call to Mark Finser at the Rudolf Steiner Foundation with the message, "We need your help in Aspen," brought Mark and his father, Siegfried, to the school to start the process of putting our economic house in order and strengthening our sense for a Waldorf community.

Never was there a more graphic example of the difference in educational approaches than that first Christmas, when I gazed down the hall at the Christmas tree of the childcare providers that shared our building. At their end was a plush, bursting tree with loads of sparkling lights and gobs of presents at its base. On our end was a "Charlie Brown" sprig cut by Kate Friesen with paper roses, planetary symbols and candles set in the branches.

"What I experienced in the first building was that we had built a temple to the sun, a color laboratory that would be a magical place in which children could grow up."

At an Avalanche Ranch retreat with the Finsers, the seriousness of the school's intention to buy land and build became apparent. At the Hotel Jerome, I met with Doug Sheffer and Bil Dunaway and a matching loan agreement was roughed out whereby the two would extend a loan to the school to purchase the land. An architect friend of mine, Nick Morrow, came from Santa Fe and spent ten days with Jeff Dickinson hammering out the conceptual details of the overall plan, incorporating all the input from the community. Later Sam Moore, an anthroposophical architect from Los Angeles, would comment that there was a living quality to the architecture due to the human hands which had shaped the building's

form. What I experienced in the first building was that we had built a temple to the sun, a color laboratory that would be a magical place in which children could grow up.

Even though I have heard it said that there wasn't a particularly strong anthroposophical impulse at the start of the school, everyone should remember the seeds that had been planted in Aspen during the 1949 Goethe Bicentennial. Those early impulses encouraged by René and Merlyn Querido lived strongly in a native Aspenite, Patty Doyle, who held much of the early anthroposophical underpinnings, along with Steven Moore. A host of Waldorf mentors have sent light and energy to the school from afar, and this school has blossomed.

"Our buildings and our community were built with love, participation and generosity."

Bob Schultz

Bob arrived in the critical third year, led the transition to the new school and is still working on his punch list.

One night in 1996, virtually every parent and supporter of the Aspen Waldorf School attended a workshop in the basement of the Yellow Brick building. It was a vision and action-setting meeting and people came prepared to make big plans and commitments. After that meeting, we had our arms around what needed to be done for the next seven years. My life work and personal economy were shaped by the vision of a campus of our own in the mid-valley. Even though for most of the participants the move was going to make things less convenient and more expensive, we were thinking way beyond ourselves and our children. It was the right thing to do.

We looked at more than a hundred sites before finding the right one, but we had already begun to think about the campus design ethic and straw-bale construction. Stephen Kanipe had been working on a new building code and had met a friend of mine, architect Jeff Dickinson. Jeff had done pioneering design work with biodomes, using Buckminster Fuller's ideas to make communities more sustainable and was now working with straw-bale construction. We knew Jeff was the right person for the Waldorf campus. His commitment to inclusion resulted in buildings that were reflective of the best of all our thinking and ideals.

We broke ground on the first building with eighteen weeks and four days until school started. No one in the valley thought we could pull it off, but we had a mission. Every time we hit a roadblock, someone or something would appear to make it dissolve.

Billy Engelman, an owner of Rocky Mountain Construction and a founding parent, offered up his best construction manager, Matt Flink. Matt worked tirelessly, side-by-side with our volunteers and hired help. He made a name for himself and now has his own successful construction business, as well as a beautiful family.

When the buildings were nearly complete, our lack of plans and funds to deal with the piles of dirt and disturbed land became a problem. As Cat Stevens asked, "Where would the children play?" Parents Jim Fox, Billy Engelman, Stephen Kanipe and Tim Fortier wanted to see a play field sooner rather than later. First, they put up the money to purchase an acre of sod and then the pipes for a future irrigation system. We called them "The Sodfathers." I called John Cerise at Grand Junction Pipe and he took measurements for the future irrigation system. He said their designer could design it in three weeks and

Jeff Dickinson teaches straw-bale construction to eager volunteers, 2000.

Bob and his daughter, Grace

have everything to us in a month. I explained that we were starting school in two weeks and wanted the pipes in a few days so that the sod could be laid before school started. He answered, "Everyone in the valley has been watching you build this school and no one can believe you're doing it. GJ Pipe is not going to be the ones to mess it up. I'll stay late tonight, design the system myself and have the parts here in two days." John also found a distributor to donate a $2,000 pump for the irrigation system. Jim, Tim and Billy laid the sod.

The final story is about the Waldorf School Community Hall. It was conceived as a 3,000 square foot common area that could also serve as a small performance space. During programming with the performance faculty, I was frustrated to see the building grow to more than 6,000 square foot – a very different and better plan than the original – but Doug Sheffer asked that instead of quibbling, we all design the building we really wanted. We had an artist make a rendering. Doug and Barbi led the effort to make that building possible. It would not

have been built without them. My observation is that the community hall is the ultimate manifestation of the building efforts. Our traditions, stories, artistic expression and community-building efforts now have a home. It is our connection to the larger community and a place to share our children's gifts.

The next phase of the school's life will be the effect our children have in the world and the growth of our academic programs. All of our focus is now on the students and teachers. I trust that it will be even more rewarding than the building phase that we just completed. Even though I am no longer a parent there, I look forward to supporting the growth of this important work. I see the benefits of this school every day as my children go through Aspen High School.

Priscilla and Jeff Dickinson

Jeff designed architectural spaces that will embrace children for the next generation. Priscilla administered the school through the building stage and through the nine-year change.

When Jeff was asked to be the architect for the new campus in Carbondale, we had no idea how significant the impact would be on our entire family. We had been watching the school from afar and had been involved in some of the early developmental stages. We were impressed by the dedication and commitment of the people involved. The only thing holding us back from our own personal involvement was the distance from Carbondale to Aspen and so it was with much enthusiasm that Jeff accepted the position of architect. When the new school opened, Priscilla accepted the position of administrator, and Sadie became a student. It was through that full immersion program that we would come to respect and honor not only the people but the teachings of Rudolf Steiner and the philosophies of Waldorf education, which matched so well with our own world views.

Sadie was not the only student at the Waldorf School on the Roaring Fork from the Dickinson family. Jeff learned about anthroposophical architecture and Priscilla learned about community development and administration. Through these experiences our careers became more enlivened and our outlook on life deepened.

The opportunity for Jeff to design the entire campus from the west wing to the community hall was an incredible opportunity to apply the concepts of sustainable design, which meshed so well with the concepts of anthroposophical design. Together they were the perfect solution to creating the best possible spaces for children. The WSRF board of trustees, by making the decision to go the route of sustainability, will have a positive impact on the lives of children for many years to come. Jeff says the Europeans set their building standards on the needs of young children who are those most likely to be affected by the materials and design of the buildings. WSRF made the right decision to hold this belief paramount.

Young Dominic Franklin lends a hand

One of Priscilla's most memorable experiences at WSRF was the building of the community hall. Through many hours of meetings on a weekly basis, each decision was reached by the building committee in a consensus manner which often was not easy but, with perseverance, was achieved. Everything from the research that was done by the various individuals to the ability to sit and listen to each other's ideas and opinions was fruit for the manifestation of something greater than themselves.

The culmination of many years of effort was brought to a head when we watched our daughter, Sadie, perform for the first time on the stage of the new community hall. It will be a moment that will be cherished forever.

*Written aboard the sailing vessel **Survival** in the West Indian Windward Islands, Leeward Islands and British Virgin Islands*

Priscilla and Jeff Dickinson stand in front of the doors to the Waldorf School Community Hall.

The door's design is based on the **Yggdrasil** (Egg-draw-sill) from Norse cosmology – The Tree of Life, The World Tree, The Heart of the World, The Heart of the Universe.

Yggdrasil is a mythological tree, formed from a tired dragon who had laid down to sleep. It stands between Heaven and Hell and embodies the nine worlds of the Norse Kingdom and represents a shift in consciousness from the divine dragon to the earthly man.

The tree's three deep taproots draw upon the Well of Fate, the Well of Knowledge and the Wellspring Hvergelmir, from which the rivers of Earth emanate providing life-force to the various kingdoms of Nature. Hvergelmir translates as the Roaring Caldron or Roaring Kettle a name similar to our valley's Roaring Fork River.

To enter the building through these doors is to sacrifice one's own self in search of knowledge, and that search ties human beings together in an immortal way.

By Doug Sheffer

See page 165 for a description of the design by the artist, Bob Johnson.

89

Building the School

**As told by
Laura Bartels-Struempler**

My first connection to Waldorf came in 1996 while building my straw-bale house on Cottonwood Pass. Though we lived in a tent, we landed regularly with Kate Friesen and Peter Westcott, old friends from environmental education encounters who were now deeply involved in the Waldorf school. Paul was two and I wasn't thinking about schools yet, but Kate began infiltrating my brain with little pieces of Waldorf and every piece fit. By the time Paul was three and we were finishing the house, I knew he needed a social encounter beyond his parents who were working alone on top of the pass. I committed to a Friday morning Mommy & Me class with CP Kanipe in Aspen, a long and worthwhile commute.

Then I learned from our friends Priscilla and Jeff Dickinson that the school was moving to Carbondale and building its first building with straw-bale. Jeff was the architect and when he said, "You have to be involved, you're the only one who knows straw-bale," I was hired as the straw boss and volunteer coordinator. I never thought it would be seven days a week with a couple of twenty-two hour days by the end of summer! It was an intense way to enter a new community and to engage in something so much bigger than I, but I fell in love with Waldorf education while talking with parents and plastering walls. The incredible commitment of this community to creating a beautiful, color-filled, textured, non-toxic, day-lit space for their children touched me. As David Orr says, it is architecture as pedagogy, what learning spaces could be. It's a concept I'm promoting in my work in natural building.

Lisa Huber measures and cuts a straw-bale

The plan for the first building process was brilliant and Matt Flink, the project manager, kept to the plan. The critical path (slab, framing, plumbing, electrical) was subbed out to professional subcontractors. The volunteer days were preplanned to work within the timeline. There was tremendous support from community members not doing construction, making lunches and offering child-care. Julie Mulcahy and Kate Friesen adopted Paul and many others.

The wall-raising for the first building was on one weekend in July of 1998. We had volunteers from the Waldorf community that extended far beyond the valley plus volunteers from the local community and the straw-bale community. We pre-trained wall captains for every section, teaching them how to pin and shape the bales and install the window bucks. There was a written, detailed plan stapled up for every section. When the weekend came, a hundred people helped to raise the walls on a 5,700 square foot building!

When it was time to stucco, though, we had a drop-dead date looming over us. I had parked my stucco machine in front of the school and one day, a lanky old man dressed in white coveralls stopped by. He said he'd been watching our progress and thought he could give us a few tips. He didn't look like an expert, but when he began talking, I could tell that he was. He had me buy a new nozzle and add Wisk laundry detergent to the mix. He taught me how to dial in the application and adjust the spray pattern. He convinced me that if we had enough people guaranteed, we could plaster the whole interior, three coats, in one weekend, and he promised he would be there beside me to walk me through it. We never learned his name but we called him the stucco angel.

Friday afternoon came. Our angel did not appear as promised. I called and called his cell phone, feeling the panic rise. Finally, he answered. He had had an inner ear infection, had lost his balance at work and fallen from a ladder. He was in the hospital; he wouldn't be with us. But we were committed. In two, twenty-two-hour days, we finished the base coats for 10,000 square feet of plaster but then we ran out of steam. It was time to call in the professionals to finish it.

Truth Window: The truth window allows the straw bales in the walls to be touched.

Building the School

Although we'd created a reasonable timeline for the campus build-out, a small group of parents persuaded us to push our timeline ahead and build the east wing the next summer. We made the decision in May and broke ground on June 21. I was the project manager and I had a blast! Not only was it empowering for me, but I felt it was empowering for all the students, especially the older girls, that a woman was in charge. They couldn't help but be moved thinking, "Our parents are building our school" and "If she can do it, I can do it."

Again, we subbed out the critical path. When Brian, the concrete subcontractor, started to use petroleum to oil his forms I stopped him, refusing to use petroleum products in the construction. We oiled the forms ourselves – using Crisco oil – and it worked! Brian was amazed. What didn't work was raising the first truss with the crane. It cracked and folded like the wings of a bird, but we pressed on and got our certificate of occupancy only eight days after school started.

The next project was the kindergarten and what we'd learned about the plasticity of straw-bale opened new possibilities for design. In order to learn all that we could about kindergartens, an aircraft was chartered and Bob Schultz, Jeff Dickinson, Doug Sheffer and I flew to San Francisco and Sacramento to visit half a dozen Waldorf kindergartens.

Every room in the school has a "truth window," a small window through the stucco that reveals the interior straw-bales. This is a straw-bale tradition, but in addition, Jeff made sure that the design of the classrooms reflected the "truth," too. The roof trusses are exposed; the vertical wall beams are on the inside of the walls. We wanted the buildings to be truly what they appear to be. This is a piece of the story of what we all did and my connection to that process. It took every single one of us without a doubt.

Bob Schultz and Stephen Kanipe, 1997

Laura Bartels-Struempler, far left, listens as Jeff teaches a lesson in straw-bale.

"I knew which group I wanted Paul to be in!"

Laura Bartels-Struempler

As project manager, Laura guided construction and especially empowered the female students.

Paul started kindergarten with Cathy Fisher and Christy Braeger in the new building and he was so happy, so fully engaged. That fall, twelve teenagers came from the Chicago Waldorf High School to help build a walkway with me as a service/class trip. At lunch, we sat together under the elm tree and talked. Nine of the twelve – despite the pink hair and pierced tongues – looked me in the eye, were well spoken, interested and interesting. Three lowered their heads and mumbled. I later learned that all of the nine had been Waldorf students from the beginning. The three had just joined the class, coming from the public schools. I knew which group I wanted Paul to be in!

I was soon asked to join the board of trustees and appreciated learning from the visionaries of the school the thoughtfulness behind their long-range plans. One brilliant aspect of the plan was that we would be able to depend less and less on volunteers for the buildings – they would burn out – and preparing for this saved us from calamity. I loved working with the board on consensus with Caroline Estes, a consultant from the Quaker community. The board works toward higher quality communication skills, new visions of money, and changing the philosophical processes from which we operate, the "three-fold social order" that Steiner envisioned. Thus, we've grown the infrastructure of the organization along with the buildings in order to form it in a way that suits our unique school. After experiencing a few angry parents and struggles with some teachers, and making many mistakes, it seems that the structure is finally working smoothly.

I chaired the long-range planning committee and worked on building and grounds until my second son, Dawson, was born in July, 2000. In March of 2001, I was badly injured in a car accident. Recovery has been slow and only last year could I again begin to participate, this time as a substitute teacher and manager of student projects. The students built every part of the planters outside their classrooms and I would like to continue to do building projects with the children. I am awed by the curriculum and the pedagogy, the sense of community and the consciousness with which most enter into and hold the community. Building the buildings, forming the community and offering the education are deeply connected.

93

I doubted...but was proved wrong.

Larry Doble

Larry made sure the building was structurally sound – and watched his daughters get a sound education.

Pam and I were involved in the school early on. I served on the board of trustees as treasurer and was active in looking for a site for the new campus. Once we started to build, my thirty years of experience in structural engineering was called upon and I was able to save the school costly mistakes and make cost-effective repairs. One I remember well was during the installation of the wooden arches in the community hall. Despite the care we were taking, the first arch was broken and I had some very specific framing communication with the company that produced the arches, to be sure it could be repaired. Now it's structurally sound and the break is invisible.

Jeff Dickinson is a great architect to work with and continues to be a friend. I have to say the same for everyone in the community. Waldorf works. Despite the endless meetings and more meetings, committees and more committees, it works. I'm proud of what we've been able to accomplish in the buildings. The campus is an enduring testimony to our efforts.

The education was actually more of a challenge and I doubted the curriculum at times, especially in reading. Both Keegan and Stella learned to read slowly and weren't really fluent until fifth or sixth grade. Now they're excellent readers, highly regarded by their literature and English teachers. Keegan is taking graduate level classes as a sophomore at the Museum of Fine Arts at Tufts University, changing her major from fine arts to art administration. Stella is thinking about the Peace Corps but actively working as a prep chef for a local caterer while she's in high school. They are self-motivated, helpful and responsible, attributes they learned at the Waldorf school. My doubts have all been proved wrong.

I enjoyed the whole process from the touching advent spiral in the Yellow Brick to the eighth grade plays. Keegan, our drama queen, was Ariel in *The Tempest*. Stella, less dramatic, did a fantastic stained glass piece for her class project. Not only my girls, but all the young people in their classes have impressed me as being extremely well-educated and well-rounded. I can say that for the adults as well. I believe in Waldorf education.

94

George Washington

"First in war, then in peace
and first in the hearts of
his countrymen."

North Atlantic

Outer Hebrides

Inner Hebrides

Scotland

Ireland

Isle of Man

Thames

Wales

England

London

Dover

English Channel

Calais

Saxons

Atlantic Ocean

Romans

Lisa Huber

Lisa learned about Waldorf with her workbelt on, enrolled her children in the school and enrolled herself in teacher training.

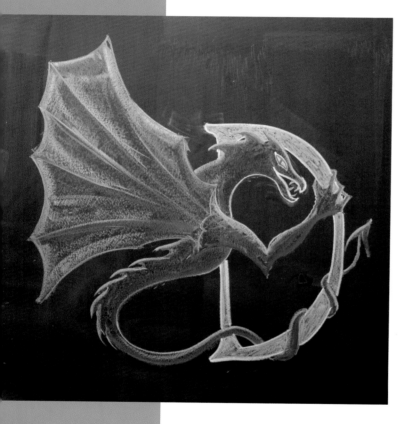

I lost my parents in a plane crash in 1966 and at 12, moved to Aspen to live with my 23-year-old sister. I was a street child, unsupervised and oddball because I didn't eat hamburgers or drink sodas and hung out with the brown rice crowd at the Grainery and Little Kitchen. After high school I moved to Glenwood, worked, and attended Colorado Mountain College. Only my uncle, a Jesuit priest, seemed to appreciate me: "You're a unique and fickle female, Lisa, but your instincts are infallible."

I met my first husband at 19, married at 22 and had Michael at 24. We were too young to know how to work out our differences. We divorced and are still friends. I married Bill Huber in 1990 and we had Marie in 1991. Both of my children were home births and my midwife was George Lilly, who is now our school secretary! Bill and I sold our Glenwood Springs homes and bought forty acres on Three-Mile Road. In our ten years there we built our home, learned a great deal about self-sufficiency, and home-schooled our children. I dug out of mud bogs up to the car doors and won the respect of my children who chanted, "Go, Mom! You can do it!"

When I saw the straw-bale school going up in Carbondale, I put on my workbelt and came to volunteer. I immediately felt connected to the parents and teachers I met and thought, "This will give my children what I cannot." During that rainy summer, René Querido came to give a talk while we sat on straw bales. Afterwards he shook my hand and said, "You're a teacher aren't you?" "Well, yes," I replied, "I've been home-schooling my children," but I knew that wasn't what he meant.

I enrolled Marie in first grade with Claire Huyghe and Michael in third grade with Frances Lewis, and I attended every parent education function. Marie's next teacher, Julie McCallan, was an inspiration to me and by the third year I assisted CP Kanipe in the kindergarten. Kindergarten was not my niche but I apprenticed with Betsy for a handwork position. That summer I enrolled in Handwork training. When Marie's class sank into crisis, I tried to go through the channels to address the problems. I met with defensiveness or non-communication at every turn and when Marie was physically hurt by a boy in her class, I said I would not risk my daughter's mental, emotional or physical well-being anymore and withdrew her from the school. I still feel sad that my concerns were not addressed. I tried to home-school and live on top of a mountain and sadly resigned my handwork position. It was heart-breaking, but I believe I was standing up for what was right and protecting my child.

I also learned at that time that Marie was severely dyslexic and no one had noticed. When she enrolled in Sopris Elementary as a fifth grader, she was mortified by the worksheets she couldn't read. We began to work with a tutor, Karen Ohlrich, now our librarian at the school, and Marie has improved greatly and is thriving at Bridges High School.

Michael began attending Glenwood Middle School, leaving the house every day with his chin up. His teachers said he was an outstanding child but he'd come home discouraged, saying, "I hate it there. Nobody's lively." When 9/11 struck and the monitors in every room were tuned to the horror all day long, I knew my children had to return to Waldorf. The faculty had changed and Kate Friesen had taken on Marie's class. Marie's self-confidence began to surge and Frances was delighted that Michael would again fill the hole he had left in her class.

"I feel I am at last on my path to self-realization."

I enrolled in Bonnie Rivers' Waldorf therapeutic and remedial training and worked as an aid for a special needs child through Mountain Boces, continuing my interest in education. In July 2002, Priscilla Dickinson astounded me by asking if I would interview to teach first grade. I thought about it, got full support from my family, and said, "Yes!" I immediately began my training at Rudolf Steiner College and am continuing in the summers with John Miles and the Micha-el Institute in Portland. I feel I am at last on my path to self-realization.

And so are my children. Michael is at Bridges High School with straight A's. He taught a workshop in geometric construction to math teachers at the Colorado Math Teachers Convention in Denver and was invited to Anaheim, California to teach at a national convention. He completed his Eagle Scout before he got his driver's license. Marie is a happy and confident eighth grade graduate. Waldorf has instilled in both of my children confidence, inner strength, perseverance and the determination to give your best. My instincts were infallible!

Charles Andrade

Artist and master Lazurist, Charles has painted the interiors of all of the school buildings over the years using the European glazing technique called Lazure.

"I am grateful to have been invited to participate with this wonderful community in the ensouling of this campus."

I was originally invited to the school to paint the first new building using the Lazure method in 1997 – initially in a workshop format. I learned Lazure in England while studying anthroposophic art and art therapy at Tobias Center for the Arts. We were taught that this unique wall treatment creates soul-nourishing environments. I have continued evolving the technique in my decorative finish business over the last twenty years and it has become one of the more popular requests that has me traveling to lazure in schools, private homes, places of worship and health centers worldwide.

Lazure painting workshops offer a valuable opportunity to build community spirit. Waldorf community members from all walks of life come together to create a nourishing learning environment for what is most important to us all, our children, our future. As such, these workshops are examples of a true social art form. When I arrived, I was amazed at how energetic everyone was. We had twenty people ready to carry the color down that long hallway. I remember how mesmerized the participants were watching me mix the colors for the Lazure glazes as if it were alchemy.

Lazure color glazing is unique to Waldorf circles. The Lazure method was indicated by Rudolf Steiner as ancillary support to the curriculum. Steiner designed the color scheme of the classrooms to work with the developmental stages the children move through from kindergarten to high school. He stated that color perception creates breathing between the etheric and astral realm. To that end, he indicated that the colors on the walls should be of a fluid, atmospheric quality where tonal hues weave through each other in a subtle manner. As the children perceive this movement, it strengthens their young souls and initiates a regenerative/healing response.

The luminous, transparent quality of lazure painting is created with glazes brushed on in layers. Lazuring is almost as if one is painting with light, using light as a pigment, etherically speaking. That light is the light of the human spirit and that's what captivates people. Science now knows that light and color are energy and that their perception actually moves down the central nervous system and back into the brain as the four qualities of color – hue, value, intensity and temperature – are taken in. Color energies are dispensed in the body where they are needed.

In July of 2002, I refurbished the rooms using an analogous color scheme that I have been developing for Waldorf schools. Although Steiner does not speak of relating the colors he recommends for the classrooms to the colors of the chakras, I have found that they

correspond almost exactly. It's another affirmation that eastern and western spiritual knowledge correspond when there is spiritual truth. In the kindergarten and early grades, we're working with the will forces or the base chakra tones and so the children are surrounded with magenta and reds. In the middle grades, we're working with the heart forces, golden-orange, yellow and green. Finally in the upper grades and high school, as the young adults' intellectual capacities come to the foreground, the turquoise, blue, lavender and peach blossom tones of the classroom offer a calming influence within which to work. Thus we work our way all around the color wheel, or up the ladder of the chakra colors, as it were. I am grateful to have been invited to participate with this wonderful community in the ensouling of this campus.

Waldorf Painting Curriculum

In the Waldorf painting curriculum, the students work with color mood as well. In the early grades the children paint the individual qualities of each color; they learn the language of color. Clothed in fairy tales and stories told to them by their teachers, the youngsters paint the expansiveness of yellow, the inwardness of blue and the dynamism of red, in this way aligning their young sensibilities to an objective quality in each hue. As they move up the grades, the color work emphasizes value and how it develops through the interplay of light and dark. In high school, the students work more consciously with the design elements of form and composition as it arises out of color and value. In their

studies of art history throughout high school, the students work with the biographies of different artists, gaining insight and encouragement in pursuing their own artistic development. The students also begin working with different paint mediums, oil and acrylic and chalk pastel, further expanding their range of expressive possibilities.

Color – and understanding it – is an integral part of the of the Waldorf environment. It is the nature and nourishment of the human soul. From the walls that gently embrace everyone who enters the buildings to the painting lessons taught in the grades and in adult painting classes, the idea that color is soul and soul is color is a vital part of the pedagogy.

Melinda Schultz

As she helped with handwork, painting and story-telling, Melinda deepened her own education.

We were living in Reno in 1992 when the house we owned in Missouri Heights caught fire. It was Bob's wish to repair it and move back to Colorado. Our neighbor there, George Lilly, told us about the new Waldorf school in Aspen. I was involved in alternative healing with a spiritual basis and the idea of a school with a spiritual basis was very appealing. We enrolled Grace in kindergarten the next year and I helped with carpooling and driving the van. When we held the Halloween Journey in 1993, I was the fortune teller and used scrying, a method I'd learned for reading crystal balls, to amaze some people with hidden truths.

When the new school was being built, I learned to lazure from Charles Andrade. He coached about twenty of us as we painted the five rooms and the hall. We used scaffolding that took us two or three levels high and we felt like Huck Finn and friends painting the fence. The first person lays on the paint, the second spreads it, the third brushes it dry working in two- to three-foot widths, high to low, and following each other in rapid succession. Each of the rooms is one hue in many shades but the hallway, of course, is a rainbow. I also layered for Charles when he painted the great mural in the hall which bewilders some people but is magnificent in all its geometric form and power. Later, Nancy Hilty and I became a lazuring team and have auctioned lazured rooms at the silent action, raising $500 to $600 for the school.

When the new school opened, Grace was in third grade, Sarah in first, and I began assisting Betsy Engelman and Kate Friesen in handwork. My favorite moments were teaching the first and second graders to knit with "Under the fence/Catch the sheep/Bring them back/Off they leap." With the older children we created the knitted farmyard which stands in the hall today. Glenn Engelman made a building and so did Matt Fox. Kelsea Mulcahy made the cabbage patch. I knitted the road. It was a great project because everyone had a part.

The next year I wrote *How the Rabbit Got Its White Coat* for Winterfaire. We transformed one of the rooms into a forest with snowy mountains and Betsy wrote the story onto boards. The children, especially the ones who were just learning to read, took turns walking through the maze, reading the story to each other. While holding the crocheted characters, the story of a fairy escaping from rats and granting the rabbit his wish of a white winter coat came to life.

Nancy and I also worked together to start the parent council, wanting it to be dedicated to the festivals and to caring for our community. I was especially active as a "good shepherd." The Good Shepherds is a committee of the parent council which helps people in need of support. I also ran the school store during festivals and made forty or fifty crocheted dolls that were donated and sold.

There were disappointments but when you send your kids to the Waldorf school, you go there too, and some of their education can be yours. I learned how to brew true English tea with Jo Richter, to lazure with Charles, to watercolor with Patty Doyle, to create handwork with Betsy, to sing more beautifully in the adult choir with Valerie Lee. My girls have surpassed the high school's expectations with their creativity and will continue to do so, but I have surpassed my own expectations as well.

"When you send your kids to the Waldorf school, you go there, too."

Ann Stahl and Mark Finser

The Rudolf Steiner Foundation (RSF Innovations in Social Finance) is linked to a network of banks and financial institutions that are seeking new ways of working with money. It facilitates transactions among donors, lenders, and receivers and helped the Waldorf School on the Roaring Fork form the pledge community that financed the construction of the new school.

Mark: I first visited the school with my father, Siegfried, in 1995. It was a special time because the school was unveiling a beautifully hand-carved sign made by John Doyle, Patty's brother, and we were there for the installation ceremony. It was also special because the founding parents realized that in order for their vision to be realized the school had to move downvalley. It was a very inspiring moment for us to see the vision for the school overriding self-interest.

Once the new site was found, a new vision for the school grew but it took enormous commitment to see it materialize. I have a memory of Ann and me traipsing around the property with the Sheffers on a cold, rainy November day. Barbi had loaned me hip boots – a nice addition to my suit and London Fog overcoat – so that we could share the vision that was coming to-gether. Barbi got stuck in the mud, tipped over, and was soon freezing. It was a picture of the sacrifices that were going to be made.

We began to speak to the school community about healthy ways to finance the cost of construction. A pledge community was formed and every school family joined in "a spirit of determined coopera-tion." People pledged what they could over a three-year period and it was this commitment that gave them the courage and confidence to build. Everyone put shoulders to the construction physically, financially and spiritually and these destiny paths, hopes and dreams are really woven into the school: straw woven into the gold of education for the next generation.

Ann: My strongest impression is contrast: How quickly it appeared – and how long the preparation time was. First, there was a little school hidden in the Yellow Brick building in Aspen and then there was the Waldorf School on the Roaring Fork!

I first visited in 1997 when Steven Moore and Patty Fox were preparing Patty's sixth grade for a eurythmy performance. I was struck by what a strong "family" they were and how comfortable they were with one another. At pre-adolescence, one doesn't often feel that comfort and it spoke to me of strength. My next visit was walking the new land and Barbi's "baptism" in the Roaring Fork River. The third visit was helping the families form their pledge community and then I remember the incredible excitement of the first straw-bale building that no one could quite believe was really there. But the culmination was that magical assembly and party blessing the community hall. It

took place in a sort of time warp in which there was a birthing of what the children had taken in over the years and could now give back. I was especially moved by the music but really, all of the adults were overcome by that assembly and the party that followed. So much has been given to the school. The challenge now will be to continue the participation with all of the families, old and new.

Mark: When Ann and I walked into the community hall in 2002, it was like walking into a musical instrument. The gifts of the children and teachers who would perform there would reverberate out into the community beyond the school, even beyond the valley.

Chapter 5

The Nine Year Change

To understand the nine year change as Rudolf Steiner describes it, whether in the life of a child or the life of an institution, one must learn a few new vocabulary words and imagine a picture of the human being not often seen. Steiner describes a four-fold human being. Only the physical body is "born" at birth. The three other bodies – etheric, astral and ego – hover around the child like loose auras to be "born" into the individual at about seven, fourteen and twenty-one.

Two imaginations may make these "bodies" more understandable. First, the *physical* body is what we have in common with the mineral world. It is the ash. The *etheric* is plant-like. It carries the life forces in its watery element. The *astral* is reflected in our instincts, our sympathies, our antipathies and our emotions. We share these feelings with the animal world. The *ego*, the higher being, belongs only to the human being.

In a second imagination, the *physical body* may be likened to a sailboat: planks, mast, wheel, etc. The *etheric body* could be likened to the water which keeps the boat afloat. For the boat to move there must be wind and this is somewhat like the *astral body*. It comes from afar and blows the boat hither and thither like a horse running freely. At last, a captain comes aboard to tame the wild winds of emotion and give the boat direction and purpose. This is the *ego*, the spiritual component of human individuality.

While the physical body is incarnated at birth, the etheric is as much a part of the world as of the child who feels he is indeed one with the world during his early years. At about seven, the etheric merges with the physical, is "born" into the body. These two bodies comprise the hereditary stream, the past, what the child has taken from the mother and father, his family tree.

The astral and ego come from afar and they bring the future potentials that are unique to the child and quite independent of heredity. The first pricks of the astral are felt at eight to nine years old and can be painful for both child and parent. Emotions bubble up without reason. The child often feels loneliness and isolation and may ask, or scream, "Are you my real parents?" "Why did you lie to me about Santa Claus?" "Don't speak to me, I want to be alone!" Parents think, "Is this adolescence, arriving at eight?"

But it is only an action-packed preview of true emotion, winds that will soon die down to blow more steadily as the astral body comes closer to the child at twelve to fourteen. Finally, the astral body fits like a cloak.

"How are emotions dealt with if there's no ego?" anxious parents may rightly ask. Until the late teens, it is the parents and other adults who must provide the ego for the growing child and this is the challenge of adolescence. Although teenagers may appear to be in charge, the captain of the ship is still learning and will stumble many times before he can reliably take the helm.

It is the initial approach of the astral body that Steiner calls the nine-year change. If parents sympathetically supply the ego forces when emotions are out of hand, the storm passes fairly quickly. The third grade curriculum provides a dependable guide with its Old Testament stories of human trial and error and divine forgiveness and the farming and building lessons. It's a time for working hard but working cooperatively, doing the chores together.

We were euphoric in September, 1997, after the raising of the bales and the "raising" of the community resulted in nearly double enrollment. But before the stucco was set, the parental and administration forms supporting the school were strained by the rapid growth. The new students brought parents whose desires and views were not always aligned with those of the parents who had been there for the school's physical or etheric birth. Finding teachers for the long term, a problem from the beginning, had yet to be resolved but here we were, having to add new classes that required new teachers.

The school structure was not complete. It wobbled on the two legs of faculty and board of trustees which were further unbalanced by intertwined roles: parents, faculty and board members were often the same people. The necessary third leg was a parent council. The families familiar with Waldorf thought they knew best what form the council should take, but enthusiastic new families felt the need to put their stamp on their school as well. Parent education that would explain the methods and philosophy of Waldorf was sorely needed, but moving the school, teaching, and trying to fit into a new skin left faculty little time for thorough discussions with parents.

The parent council had a difficult birth. In late spring the decision was made to build two rooms of the east wing a year ahead of the build-out schedule to accommodate an uncombined first grade. Laura Bartels-Struempler was the straw boss and she accomplished a monumental task in spite of reduced enthusiasm from parents who had put in an all-out effort the summer before.

The impact of the rapid building up of the school's physical body, the reforming of its etheric organizing principles, and the influx of new students and new parents that profoundly changed its soul, or astral life, made for a tumultuous nine-year-old change.

Our school was the nine-year-old, undergoing a difficult transformation, like a child poised between heredity and individuality, past and future.

Eugene Schwartz has said that often, the more difficulties a child faces at ages nine to ten, the more genial will his or her adolescence be. WSRF has risen to the challenge of proving that its communal and spiritual strength is the equal of its impressive physical being; the teenage years look bright.

Ericka Crampton, Katie Taylor and Vallee Noone at Lake Powell

107

Nancy and Jack Hilty

Nancy and Jack helped the school move on after the crisis of 1999.

The year before the school moved from Aspen, our son Max was in first grade at the Carbondale Community School. It wasn't what we had hoped for so at the Schultz's suggestion, we drove Max and our daughter, Summer, to Aspen to check out Frances Lewis' first and second grade class. We walked into their play practice and it took one minute to decide. This was it. This was the teacher and the school we wanted for Max for eight years.

Plans were already underway for the move to Carbondale. We attended the ground-breaking ceremony and before we knew it, we were stacking straw-bales. The more we learned about the art-based approach to the education, the better we liked it. (Nancy works in color and clay, Jack in marble.) When Nancy attended the workshop with Charles Andrade, she fell in love with lazuring, blown away by all the color.

Nancy: Max started second grade with Frances and the next year Summer started kindergarten with Helena Hurrell. They both loved school, but it was a difficult time for the adults. We were trying to start a parent council but didn't have experience working with consensus. Robert Schiappacasse, administrator of the Shining Mountain Waldorf School in Boulder, came up to describe the typical organization of a Waldorf school. The parent association, he said, was all of the parents in the school. Within that group, the parent council was to be made up of representatives from each class either selected by the teachers or elected by the class parents. The council would then elect their board and a representative to the board of trustees. While we were attempting to do this, one new parent supported by a few others appointed himself to the board of trustees without due process. We had a struggle to manage this and keep moving forward. Melinda Schultz and I co-chaired the first parent council founded in due process and using consensus.

This took a lot of energy. I think parents get so passionate about Waldorf education that strong, creative impulses bubble up and they think their ideas should be incorporated into the structure. During those first years in Carbondale, there wasn't enough form to hold the ideas in place and it was not a healthy situation. I think, too, the school was desperate for enrollment and we weren't able to say, "The Waldorf school may not be the right place for you." Now we're clearer about what we are and what we are not.

Jack: I just observed for the first three years, picking up the philosophy from Frances and Max. We loved the depth of the teachings, the beautiful drawings, the color saturated into his main lesson books. It was wonderful to watch his awareness awaken. When I was asked to become involved in the governance, I felt I didn't know enough but worked first on the finance committee and then the board. I saw the struggle behind the scenes, what it takes to keep things going, and the parents who thought about the school twenty-four hours a day. There were times when it felt like we were living out of a tent, one crisis away from collapse, but the staying power of parents who want this improved education is amazing.

I've tried to forge a path for businesses to support the school by donating a portion of my fees for orthodontics for Waldorf students back to the school. I say, "I know more about orthodontics than selling cookies," and I hope other parents and friends of the school will begin to donate their profits of one days' construction or medicine or law practice to help underwrite the cost of Waldorf education.

"The staying power of parents who want this improved education is amazing."

Jennifer Schiller

Jennifer jumped in to carry the school through the first difficult years in the mid-valley.

I've had my ups and downs with the school as we all have. There have been times when I've thought, "Was this a huge, expensive, brain-damaging, time-consuming mistake?" It was hard to write a check for $1,000 every month and have both children come home saying they hated school. But when I walk in there today, the feelings I had when I first walked in six years ago are still there and now we're deliriously happy with Jon's transition to high school. He grew up in that garden, that soil. Beyond the curriculum he got to avoid drugs, guns and pop culture. He had best friends and we had "best families."

I first visited when the new school opened in Carbondale with four classes and Cathy Fisher in the kindergarten. I was looking for a place for Tori that would be more than a daycare and I couldn't believe what I saw. How could Cathy maintain order in that pile of five-year-olds without raising her voice or giving orders? They just followed her, busy, chattering, happy, but under her spell. And it smelled so good! I had been volunteering in Jon's second grade class at Basalt Elementary and the contrast was astounding: no screaming, no running, just peaceful energy. I thought, "If I feel like this, how beneficial will it be for my children?"

"We took the leap of faith."

I started hanging around, helping with Mayfaire, and the next year, we took the leap of faith not knowing where the money for tuition was going to come from. Jon joined Frances Lewis' class but he wasn't a kid who made us realize what a wonderful decision we'd made. It wasn't until parent night that we had the first shining moment. When I commented on his main lesson book he said, "I really like my main lesson book." "Why?" I asked. "Because it's beautiful." Here was a child who really hadn't shown up for school saying his work was beautiful. "Yes!" we thought, "It was a good choice." Still, we were mostly discouraged about his reaction. He was invested in not liking school and we thought we had the child who was going to finally embarrass the whole Waldorf community.

Tori was the opposite. She loved school. From the beginning, when we learned that Cathy could move those kids around because she used "rhythm, ritual and repetition" in the kindergarten, we started changing things at home, saying blessings at meals, lighting candles at bedtime, turning off the TV. There was a dramatic change in our house. I'd read a lot of parenting books, but they all say, "Do this, do that, and the kids will turn out OK." They disregard your unique kid! I read *The Family Guide to Waldorf Education* when they enrolled and the articles on the temperaments (choleric, phlegmatic, sanguine and melancholic) finally explained to me why, when I insisted Jon do something in my choleric way, he just dug in his phlegmatic heels.

Still, we were disappointed that Jon didn't seem to "get" the medieval period or Norse mythology. By the end of 7th grade, he just wouldn't go back and we were tired of rolling the Sisyphus boulder up the hill. We enrolled him in Basalt Middle School where we were a bit surprised that he passed all the tests with flying colors. A month later he said, "Mom, could I go back to the Waldorf school for one last year?" He just needed to make his own decision without his choleric mother on his case. In retrospect he says he's glad he went to the Waldorf school. At Bridges High School, he recently flew through a paper on medieval history and not long ago, when he and his Waldorf friends were listening to a CD of John Williams' music, I said, "Did you know that Williams was influenced by Wagner?" They answered, "Oh, yes. And Wagner was influenced by the Norse myths and so was J.R.R. Tolkein." When we watch a movie together, he gets the references to *Beowulf*, *Moby Dick*, Shakespeare, Gilbert and Sullivan. He did get it! He sees how we're all connected in all sorts of ways.

I didn't know it at the time but what I wanted for my kids was a classical education and they got one. But beyond that, in the space created by the students, teachers, families, the kids get to be who they really are and so do I! At Mayfaire, when I dress in my Renaissance gown and put on my flower crown, I think, "This is who I'm meant to be!" There are all sorts of kids now at Bridges and my son can look at others and know which ones are safe to hang out with, which ones are not. Life isn't about being cool and hip, it's about showing up and being who you are.

The Temperaments

One of Steiner's insights for which Waldorf parents are especially grateful is that of the temperaments. Nowhere else in popular child development literature are they fully described. Understanding the temperaments, particularly of children between seven and fourteen, can be as helpful in the home as it is in the classroom.

The temperaments blend the stream of heredity, carried in the physical and etheric bodies, with the stream of individuality carried in the astral body and ego. In each unique child, one of these bodies predominates much like the moods of the four seasons or the colors of the color wheel.

The melancholic child, tall and lean, is most attached to the physical body. He often exhibits a contemplative, fall mood and might be said to see the world through a mauve glass. He is often alone, often serious, and concerned with the meaning of things, how things die away, the bones that remain. While the melancholic might be self-absorbed, even self-pitying, he can also be of the greatest service to humankind, a doctor or social worker, quintessentially an Abe Lincoln. Melancholics are also the best comedians: Charlie Chaplin, Marcel Marceau.

Ben Liotta, candlemaker

The opposite is true of the sanguine, the spring child. She is light-hearted, fleet-footed, smiling and delightful. She learns quickly – and forgets quickly – as she flits like a butterfly from flower to flower, from friend to friend. She loves everyone equally and perhaps superficially but is socially aware and caring and makes everything fun. She has organizational gifts that are not always apparent and when she's happy, as she usually is, her mood blows over the group like a warm astral breeze.

As the first yellow of spring ripens into the blood-red of summer, so the fiery choleric child shouts her arrival. She is ready for action, perhaps destructive action, but like a little Napoleon, the choleric, ego-dominated, charges into the future. She forgets at times the wishes or feelings of others and can be dictatorial – or a selfless leader like Winston Churchill. The choleric starts new enterprises, new schools.

Phlegmatics are connected with the blue, watery elements of the etheric body. These winter children are comfort-loving, food-loving, round and kind and sociable. They are loyal friends, great hosts and the heart of any group. Although phlegmatics can be lazy, still waters run deep and they can surprise you with penetrating actions and ideas. Sometimes these ideas scour out a deep channel that is very difficult to change and the phlegmatic becomes obstinate. At other times, unexpected storms sweep across the waters.

Thus, each of the four temperaments has a positive and a negative side and it is important to work with the child toward the strengths of his temperament and not attempt to change the temperament or make it seem a fault. Further, while one temperament may predominate, no temperament stands alone. They all blend like colors on a color wheel or the seasons of the year and so we can find balance in the neighboring temperaments.

A child makes progress by experiencing one temperament to the fullest extent possible until he or she is ready to move on to the next. A young school may often evince this tendency, as well. The emotional well-being of an adult, however, comes about when all four temperaments are in balance, each ready to be utilized "upon demand." As it approaches its next phases of growth and development, the Waldorf School on the Roaring Fork is striving to achieve such a balance.

*This description of the temperaments is indebted to René M. Querido's in **Creativity in Education, the Waldorf Approach**.*

Catherine Woolcott

"For the loving, unconditional and selfless gift the teachers have given my daughters, I am eternally grateful."

Catherine has bridged the parent-teacher purview with her work on parent council, board of trustees, faculty and community council.

My husband Rick and I lived most of our lives in San Diego, close to family and friends. But when our first-born, Katelyn, began first grade at the same elementary school I attended as a child, I began to wonder, "Is this all there is for me, for my children?" So when Rick was offered a position teaching special education at Yampah Mountain High School in Glenwood Springs the summer of 1997, we saw it as an opportunity to experience life at a slower pace in a smaller town.

For all of the positives in our new life, we never anticipated Katelyn's change in spirit when she started at the public school. This happy, social child became more interested in going on walks alone than with the family, showed little interest in her baby sister Claire, and would no longer join us in Grace at dinner or prayers at bedtime. We were told she was a model student, but deep down we knew some part of her was not being reached the way she needed. We knew of no other options, but took her out of school and began to look. It was then we learned that the Waldorf school had just moved thirty miles closer to us in Carbondale. Katelyn visited Frances Lewis' class and skipped out after her first day looking as if she had always been there. I was moved to tears to see something back in Katelyn I had not seen in a long time. While she played in the dirt pile, climbed trees and shared lunch with her new friends, I toured the school with Jenny Strube-Callihan and Kathryn King, from whom I immediately felt warmth and acceptance. Kathryn became a mentor to me that day and many conversations ensued on how the Waldorf curriculum meets the child in developmentally appropriate ways, and how deeply beauty and truth are woven into the fiber of all that is brought to the children. I was, and continue to be, touched by my children's days, the beauty of the school, and the integrity of the faculty and staff who stand before them.

Katelyn had a rich six and a half years in the grade school, while Claire had her beginning in the garden with Keith Schlussler, the biodynamic gardener, and his dog, Osso. When Claire turned three the following fall, she joined Christy Braeger's Flying Fish Preschool, which we still think may be the best year of her life!

It was not long before I was asked to be on the tuition assistance committee. Here I could participate in making this tremendous education available to families who, like us, may not otherwise have the resources to consider an independent school.

Through the years I have served in a variety of capacities, from class parent and board of trustees member to founder of the school store, to joining the interim task force from which the community council was born. In the past four years, I feel the community council has been the most challenging and rewarding work I've done and the best fit for the gifts I bring. For a while, everything was channeled through the council and my treasured memories are of the camaraderie, tears and joys of working with people with whom I would trust my life. Yes, we have made mistakes. We have unwittingly participated in hurt feelings as families and teachers have transitioned from the school, but with our best intentions intact, we have continued to grow, learn and mature.

Dominic Franklin and Marie Huber

In 2003, Sigrid Fischbacher and I co-taught the kindergarten, but I became ill and despite receiving an outpouring of love from the community, I could not return as a teacher. I have now returned to work as the director of the kindergarten and I continue to manage A Child's Cup of Tea, the school store Julie Mulcahy and I started in 1998. I see kindergarten parents now who really seem to understand what their children are receiving and who know what they want for their families.

My thoughts and feelings regarding my experience at the Waldorf School on the Roaring Fork were further crystallized at Katelyn's eighth grade play last spring. She was Rosalin in *As You Like It* and as she gave her closing monologue standing tall and alone in front of closed curtains, I saw a young lady inspired with the poise and confidence to meet the future with enthusiasm. I sat there and reflected on the many times Frances Lewis, Holly Richardson or Lyman Jackson held a light, bright and loving picture of Katelyn when I found it too challenging – and now I have the privilege of having Julianna Lichatz doing the same for us with Claire. For the loving, unconditional and selfless gift the teachers have given my daughters, I am eternally grateful.

Christy Braeger

Christy came for her children and stayed to become a teacher.

As I ponder my Waldorf story, a sense of awe and wonder surrounds me. We, who assisted in the early years of the school, were given opportunities to stretch, strive and grow beyond what we thought possible. We joined the school in its third year and now my two children are eighth grade Waldorf graduates and I am a lead kindergarten teacher with a class of twenty.

Our journey began with my search for educational inspiration for my own children. Public school presented problems; I began to search for answers. The Lallier family, our Glenwood Springs neighbor and founding parents, planted the initial seeds of curiosity. I was fascinated with the wood play stands and their daughter's skills and imaginative play. I soon found myself

attending lectures and festivals on the periphery of the small Waldorf school initiative that was taking root in Aspen. Unable to meet the financial criteria, I continued to dream and hope. Then, at a workshop in Carbondale in 1994, I was touched first by walking through a five point star in eurythmy, then by my daughter's tenacious grip on her grass doll, which CP Kanipe helped her make and finally by words that resonated in my soul. "We would like you to join our school and we can offer a workable financial picture." I had no idea that this was a transformation for me as well as a beginning for my children.

Dustin began in a combined first and second grade class of nine children, with Patty Doyle as his teacher. Chandra started kindergarten with CP Kanipe and her assistant, Ms Allen, with a class of ten students. The songs, stories and reverence which my children brought into our home drew me to the school. In 1995, I began my employment at the Aspen Waldorf School. Each day was busy as I worked in the office, assisted CP Kanipe in the kindergarten as an aftercare provider and drove the down-valley bus. We were up at 5:00 a.m. to pick up the first children in Glenwood Springs and begin the 100 mile round trip commute. We were home at 5:00 p.m. when road construction did not interfere.

In 1996, our family moved to El Jebel and I was asked to assist Cathy Fisher in our first satellite kindergarten at the Blue Lake Community Center. Though the location was ideal, the space was high-maintenance as we had to pack up every weekend so it could be used for church services and other activities. In the summer we provided childcare for parent volunteers building the new school. Our spare time was given to cutting and stacking straw bales and learning to lazure and stucco. In 1997, at the close of summer, the new building was finished. Cathy and I gathered supplies to open the new on-campus kindergarten.

The next year, there was a demand for a program for younger children and the Horace Work family offered their rental house on Flying Fish Road, less than a quarter of a mile from the school. Our family moved into the home and The Children's Garden, a Waldorf inspired preschool, was born. The work load was a bit intimidating. The five acres had been left to nature with overgrown grass, no fencing and a few neighbors who were concerned about the impact the school would have on their rural neighborhood. My own children worked endlessly sanding, moving rocks, mowing and painting. Though the school would help with the supplies and the observation of other Waldorf home programs, legal issues prevented them from employing me. In addition, opening The Children's Garden was contingent upon a fenced yard, other modifications and a ream of licensing approvals. The task was at times larger than life, but the generous help of the Sheffers and many others saved the day and we opened on time with full enrollment.

We participated in festivals and special events at the main campus but otherwise we were quite independent with our cockatiels, ducks, bunnies, hamsters and a dog. The joyful children and animals were full of life, but life requires extensive maintenance. As a single mom, I depended on my children to mow the two acres, feed and clean animal cages and help me prepare for each busy week. In winter, unprepared for plowing, we shoveled our long country driveway to allow easy drop-off for childcare. After two years, the Works decided to sell their house. It was sad to see The Children's Garden close but I was glad to follow my pre-schoolers to the newly built Early Learning Center at the WSRF. Rebecca Raine asked me to be her assistant. I accepted and began preparations for my third kindergarten initiative. I sewed new curtains, napkins and placemats and helped clean up from the construction.

The following year the community encouraged me to apply for the lead teaching position. In 2001 through 2003, I was the lead kindergarten teacher with James Tonnozzi as my assistant. We became a cohesive team and filled our classroom with an enriching Waldorf curriculum but when my father was ailing in 2003, Dustin, Chandra and I made plans to return to Wisconsin, which I'd always thought of as home.

After fond good-byes to our school community, we drove to Wisconsin only to realize that our "home" was in Colorado. Weeks after we returned to Colorado my desire to be with children reunited me with WSRF once again. I was hired as the lead aftercare teacher, asked to do some mentoring and to work in the morning program. In 2004 I resumed my position as a lead kindergarten teacher.

I little suspected that I would be a part of four Waldorf preschool-kindergarten initiatives or have the privilege of assisting three remarkable kindergarten teachers. I have the honor of observing beauty and reverence through the work of one remarkable angelic assistant and have met a family who has taught me unconditional giving. The heartfelt gestures extended to me and my family will continue to put a lump in my throat, bring a tear to my eyes and instill my work with a light-filled pulse. Blessings to you all. Twelve years later, I'm honored and humbled to be a gardener among the lives of children.

Movement Education

by Julianna Lichatz with Kim LeBas

As with all other aspects of the Waldorf curriculum, the movement program meets the growing individual with a developmental approach while maintaining a sense for the good, the beautiful and the true. In the early years, all subjects are introduced through movement. After an active introduction, subjects are taught through feelings and images. Spiritual forces arise within the soul to engender thoughtful understanding only after the "hands" and "heart" have been engaged.

Rhianna Borderick and Malia Machado

Before seven, imitation is the guiding principle. Children strengthen their growing physical bodies through an inner motivation to love and imitate the adults around them. In the Waldorf kindergarten, they imitate sanding wood, hammering and sawing, kneading bread, washing laundry, digging, weeding and planting. They run, skip, leap, chase, jump, clap, catch and throw in natural movement during circle. Besides developing large motor skills, early childhood teachers work with finger plays to assist the young child in entering into his fingers with fine motor skills.

In grades one through five, children inhabit the world of imagination and rhythm. Games begin with the circle, a symbol for wholeness and unity, holding the child safely and securely, protected by the group. In grade two, we begin to dispel the circle, gradually asking children to step outside and stand alone. In third grade, the children cross a significant bridge, experiencing their own bodies and egos as separate from the group. At the same time, they enter a more social world. Physical orientation, directionality, coordination and dexterity help children find themselves in the world physically, socially and emotionally.

The games and activities for these grades are found on back stoops, fields and playgrounds handed down from generation to generation in all of the world's cultures. Deep wisdom lies hidden in hide-and-seek, tag, jump rope, London Bridge, Ring around the Rosie and hopscotch, games in which there is a strong emphasis on physical orientation – right/left, above/below, back/front – which is dependent on the self/center.

In the middle school years, sports are introduced, as well as fencing, Bothmer exercises, ball skills, group challenges, circus arts and gymnastics skills. In sixth grade, emphasis is placed on learning through cooperation. In seventh, students want and need to take risks through problemsolving. Teamwork and the development of strategies dominate eighth grade games.

Throughout the curriculum we allow children to play with, explore and define three-dimensional space, which is alive with laws of its own. It is frequently observed that Waldorf graduates become outstanding athletes even though they are not encouraged to participate in sports at an early age. The movement program and eurythmy teach the dynamics of space. Students learn to develop and spiritualize the space they inhabit in harmony with the others around them. In the early grades, we gently move the child from the peripheral world – with which he feels united – to experience the self in the center. At puberty, the process is reversed. We encourage the young person to move from self-interest to interest in the world. This is done not through words but through movement, through games.

119

Holly Richardson

Holly scooped up Robin Marcus' class, carried them through graduation, and will be serving the school well into the new millennium.

"It takes some people their whole lives to find their path but I found mine right away."

I always knew that I wanted to be in education. I was a good student and adored my teachers. When I was student body president of the largest high school in North Carolina, I had a principal who gave me complete freedom and inspired me to raise school spirit, getting everyone involved. I so admired her and thought, "That's what I want to do."

I first met Waldorf education through my sorority housemother whose little apartment was covered with angels. She told me about the Findhorn Community in Scotland and gave me books to read. When I met Frances Lewis, first my running partner and soon my good friend, I read my books to her about how each of us was like a shining star in the heavens – and we decided then to start our own school!

But after college I went as far away as I could, to Eugene, Oregon, to run political campaigns for the Sierra Club. Venus, one of the many "alternative" people I met, took me to the Waldorf school there. The school was closed but the bookstore was open and I bought some books – which are still on my bookshelf, unread. But I felt butterflies. There was a feel to the school that touched me and I kept it in my back pocket.

After two years of campaigning in Oregon, I was burned out and my brother, Ty, told me to come to Aspen and talk to his good friend, Patty Doyle, a local teacher. I called her and then tracked down my old friend Frances, who was also in Aspen, to find that Frances had just been hired by Patty and the Aspen Waldorf School faculty as the new first grade teacher! I arrived, walked into the Aspen Waldorf School and felt I had walked home. I moved in with Fran and volunteered at the school helping with aftercare, office work and field trips. I joined a study group with Steven Moore, Barbara Allen, Kathryn King, Barbi Sheffer and Burnsie, Carla Beebe Comey's future husband. We read *Christianity as Mystical Fact* and I was so taken by it that I knew I had to do the teacher training. I chose Emerson College and moved to England in 1998 just as the Aspen school became the Waldorf School on the Roaring Fork and moved to Carbondale.

My foundation year was profound and hard to describe, but everything seemed to speak to me directly, answering my questions about life and its meaning, carrying my thoughts further. During my second year, I learned the Carbondale school was in crisis. That summer, Frances came to Europe to travel with me and we talked about the school. She never put any pressure on me but when I said I'd like to come for an interview, she could hardly believe she didn't have to kidnap me – as she'd been instructed to do.

Coming over Independence Pass, Frances and I stopped to jump into the Punch Bowl, a sort of symbolic "jumping in with both feet," and when we got to the school, that's what I did. I was amazed to see what had been built since I had attended the ground-breaking but when I stood before the combined sixth/seventh grade class that I'd inherited from Robin Marcus and Patty Doyle, I realized how little I'd learned. Though I was excited and scared, I connected instantly with those kids. We hiked to the top of Mount Sopris together and just went to work. When my own parents moved here, I felt so supported. Everyone – parents, colleagues, students and my family – wanted me to succeed.

Meeting and marrying my husband, Dan, is interwoven into the story, too. My father met Dan, liked him instantly and told him he should meet his daughter who taught at the Waldorf school. Dan wasn't so sure but he knew the Kanipes, had interned with Stephen, and when they, too, recommended me, he came to the school and peeked in my classroom window to check me out. It took him a month to call for a Friday date, but that afternoon he came into my classroom to shake my hand – and set the children all dancing around him. I thought, "I have met my match today," and when he proposed some months later, he did it in my "home," my school classroom.

I proudly graduated my two classes and then helped Frances with her classes until my pregnancy required bed rest. Now, being a mother has made Waldorf even more beautiful and more important. In the beginning, I just loved it and my involvement was selfless, pure heart. Now I'm motivated in a new way to build the school for the future. I'm teaching a parent/child workshop, work that is so important and that I never thought twice about before. Someday, when my children are there, I'll go back to work full-time. It takes some people their whole lives to find their path but I found mine right away.

A Performance Hall Built Like a Musical Instrument

The community hall was completed in February of 2002 and celebrated on April 6 with performances by the classes, dinner, dancing, toasts and speeches. Almost everyone who had been involved in the founding, financing, bale-raising and nail-driving was invited and all who were there felt that a magical space had been created. It would welcome visitors to coffee and conversation in the sun room, give the administration and board of trustees space for consensus meetings and provide faculty with desperately needed workspace.

Eurythmy would have an embracing space of its own. But most importantly, the stunning plays and eurythmy performances directed by Steven Moore and the music and concerts conducted by Valerie Lee would have a venue worthy of their virtuosity. The performance hall housed within this building was later named after Steven Moore. All felt that a sounding forth would ring through the valley from this beautiful performance hall which had been "built like a musical instrument."

Indeed, every play and performance continues to bring the community together in further celebration. Not only can parents finally see and hear their children perform, but they can enjoy themselves as a community afterwards, sharing special moments in the planning, preparation and performance, telling anecdotes and absorbing compliments.

The hall was built, in a sense, to honor the work of Steven Moore, speech, drama and eurythmy teacher for more than a decade. It became as well a worthy space for the memorial service held for him on April 6, 2004.

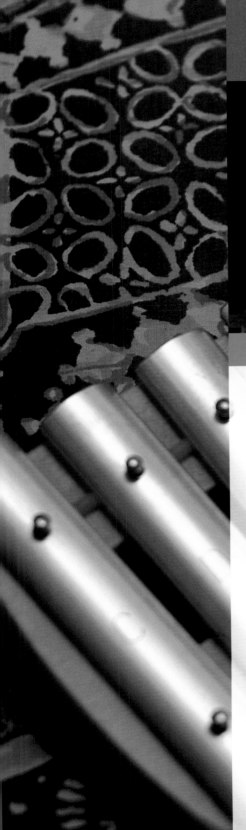

Chuck Cole

Chuck began as a parent, served as contractor for the community hall and was the first board president who was not a founder.

I've been on the board of trustees for five years and the board president for three but now I've stepped down. When I took over I said to Barbi and Doug Sheffer, "I'll do this but you're not going anywhere!" I needed their history. I was the second generation, the builders. Now we're bringing new people on to the board; what I call the third generation parents who weren't founders or builders but who will lead the school through its adolescence.

My wife, Summer, and I enrolled our children, Matthew and Mackenzie, in Cathy Fisher's Children's Garden in Blue Lake when it opened in 1995. When the school moved, we were there to help. I was working for Aspen Earthmoving during construction of the first three buildings and they were very generous with the equipment for hauling and excavation that I used as a volunteer on weekends. Because I'd wanted to start my own construction business for several years, I expressed interest when we started planning the community hall. I was invited onto the design committee and the next thing I knew, I'd quit my job at Aspen Earthmoving and had my first contract, a $1.6 million job! But you know, it came in on budget and on time.

The design committee included Steven Moore, Valerie Lee, Priscilla and Jeff Dickinson, Bob Schultz, Robert Schiller and Doug Sheffer. I was there when Doug decided we had to see the Pine Hill Waldorf School auditorium. We met at 6:30 a.m. on the tarmac at Aspen airport, boarded a Lear jet and flew to New Hampshire! After we landed, the pilot surprised us by saying he had to be back on the ground in Aspen by 7:00 p.m., which left us about two hours to tour. We looked at the auditorium and school, asked our questions, got ideas about what we wanted and what we didn't.

Jeff Dickinson and Bob Schultz

"The community hall isn't a building, it's a piece of art!"

124

Before the trip we'd had a lot of discussions about sizing. Steven and Valerie felt that the floor of the eurythmy room, the stage and the auditorium should hold twenty-four children in a thirty-two foot diameter circle so that whatever they practiced and staged could be moved without reconfiguring it. In the jet on the way back Doug, Jeff, and Bob started playing the card game, Euchre, against Steven and Val, who didn't know the game and were playing intuitively. To make it more interesting, Bob suggested they make the stakes square footage, and by the end of the flight Steven and Val had a venue for their grand performances! It was a great trip – crazy – but it helped us move our design forward, or as Valerie said, "to dream energetically." Size wasn't the only design change. We added a sophisticated lighting, sound and video system and office equipment because when you get a crazy guy like Doug who loves theater and has the ability to outfit it, magical things happen.

The design committee was trying to pick the colors for the sound fabric under the slats on the wall and in the curtains and was leaning toward a sea green. Valerie thought, "Oh no, too cold." Melinda, Maureen and Emily came in and said, "You've got to have red if it's a theater!" And that's how the gorgeous red came about.

We were scheduled to break ground the first week in June as soon as school was out, but being impatient to start, I cut a few trees the last days of school. Some of the older kids were very upset because they thought of these trees as pets. I had to cut the trunks of those trees into three-inch discs so that each student could take one home! That was almost, but not quite, the only real trouble we had on the job. I dug the hole for the foundation a few days later and when the concrete crew showed up we had two feet of crystal clear water in the hole – a swimming pool! They'd turned on the irrigation across the road and we'd pierced the water table. I went back to Aspen Earthmoving and got a 6,000 gallon-a-minute pump. We poured concrete a day later and kept the pump running all summer. We now have a built-in de-watering system that runs from June to October.

All the members of the design and building team were friends. It was important to us that we work out of consensus, and building the community hall was the most harmonious experience you can imagine. You can see the evolution of Jeff Dickinson, architect, from one end of the school to the other, but this was my first job so we came to the project with different ideas and backgrounds. Still, we had an intuitive sense with one another. There were places where I knew his way would turn out best and I'd step back, other places where he did. Larry Doble, another parent, was our engineer. He'd come out, listen to my ideas, and if he thought they'd work, he said yes.

When the sub-contractors started in July, we made "school" rules: no smoking (especially because it was straw-bale!), no loud or inappropriate music, no foul language. With one exception, a framer who liked his acid rock, the subs thought it was a great place to work and you can see in the building that some were unique artists in finish carpentry and painting. There are a few flaws that drive me crazy – no one else knows they exist – but because I was among friends and it was our school, I got to go about the project like an owner. It felt then and still feels like my own house and a lot of people are as comfortable there as I am.

When the straw came, we parked our two big truckloads on the frontage road and Bob Schultz posted our bale-raising days on the Internet. We had people from all over the valley – and the world, even the Netherlands! – coming to help. Being on the highway, the whole community could watch the straw being transformed into a building. I left a set of prints out whenever we had volunteer days so everyone could sign them, then I sealed them in a plastic tube and buried them under the building. They'll be there for the next millennium. The community hall isn't a building, it's a piece of art. New parents walk on to the campus and they don't have to know anything about Waldorf education to be attracted. When they start to educate themselves about the kind of education we offer, they get it.

My personal growth from working with this organization is immeasurable. When I joined the board, I thought I'd know what to do. I had to learn to listen, listen, listen – and then to ponder. So many times I've changed my direction after hearing all sides to the issue. Steiner says every issue has twelve points of view and now I believe it! It's changed how I run my business and how I relate to everybody in my life.

It's amazing to me that our school has gone through every stage that Steiner described for the growing child: the challenges of the third year, the ninth year, the twelfth year. When a master teacher from Highland Hall in Northridge, a fifty-year-old suburban Los Angeles Waldorf school, came to speak to us recently, he assured us that challenges aren't going to go away. We've got to be loving enough to support and encourage people when we're going through an issue and bold enough not to brush it under the rug. I think the second generation has learned how to do this better than the first. Our buzzwords have been "follow through" because there are always people who can't bring their issue to the person involved. They talk about it in the parking lot thinking, "If I say this to enough people, someone will pay attention." We've got to address those issues right away. For a while there were so many issues the mentoring support team couldn't answer them all and the community council had to help.

The community council has been a good model while we've built our faculty. In the Waldorf movement, there's a demand for more than two hundred new teachers every year and maybe forty trainees, so you have to come up with your own faculty. We're now paying an untrained teacher an associate teacher's wage but we budget them as trained and spend the difference sending them to training. The faculty is getting stronger every year and there's talk of starting a college of teachers, which broadens the teachers' responsibility for the school and deepens their level of study. I think it's the right transition to adolescence.

Robert Schiller

Robert found his work on the board of trustees a challenge on many levels.

Jennifer and I weren't happy with Jon's public school experience through second grade and our daughter, Tori, had outgrown her preschool but wasn't old enough yet for kindergarten. Searching for alternatives, we visited the Waldorf School on the Roaring Fork at their first Mayfaire in Carbondale and then toured during an open house. In addition to the natural setting of the campus, we were impressed by how the performing arts, which had always been central to our lives, were woven through the curriculum. Here was a school that thought more about nurturing healthy, well-rounded human beings than about test scores and employability.

From the start, Jennifer participated actively in the school while I stayed in the background. I don't think we had been involved for more than two years when, during a ski club barbecue at Snowmass, I sat with Barbi and Doug Sheffer. To my surprise they asked me to consider joining the board of trustees. After some self-examination I accepted and came to understand how important education is in the life of a child and a family, and how "life and death" the issues involved in running a school can be. It was as challenging as anything I've ever done in my personal or working life. I often felt like an amateur facing the concerns that were brought to us.

"I helped to move things forward when a question or challenge threatened to obstruct the progress."

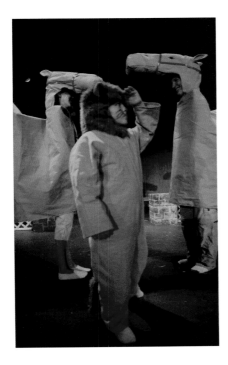

I quickly discovered the realities of the financial life of the school and saw how deeply indebted we were to the Sheffers' support. When I found out what the teachers were paid, my first reaction was, "How can they live on that?" It was quite an eye opener. The board has continued to try to close the gap between income and outgo but it is difficult. A Waldorf education is probably always going to appeal to only a particular segment of the population, and this valley is a small pool from which to draw.

Even before joining the Board, I had enjoyed volunteering to help construct the Early Learning Center, stacking bales and painting walls. As an architect and manager of large projects, there's no hands-on in my daily work so to be out there participating was fun. When the community hall was being planned, I served on the building committee. One of the remarkable things about the school is how ideas develop out of one person's vision, then branch out, are worked on by more people and become something greater than anyone foresaw. Once the community hall was under construction, I had the chance to get my hands dirty once again, this time running the stucco machine and spreading the plaster with my son, Jon. That's one of many precious memories we will always have.

Another memory is when the community hall design committee was wondering how we could possibly raise the $1.7 million it was going to cost. Doug very quietly said something to the effect of "I think we have that covered," to which we all responded with a rather stunned silence as it dawned on us that he meant he and Barbi would provide the money. In my own practice, I've observed clients blithely spending hundreds of thousands, even millions of dollars for their own gratification, but to witness someone making that kind of a commitment for the benefit of others was a totally different gesture and a reminder of the good that people can do.

The completion of the hall fulfilled everyone's expectations, and several celebratory events brought the community together in a way that had previously been impossible because of space. Unlike, say, a church congregation, where people see each other every week, we'd had little opportunity to gather and feel like a community because we didn't have a suitable space. Now we did. Attending the children's first plays on the new stage was especially gratifying given the importance of performance in bringing our family to the school.

The Waldorf School on the Roaring Fork has helped to mold our children, but it has also reshaped our family and the choices we make in our lives. We turned off the TV, read more books, wrote, painted, played music, sang and established deep new friendships. Our involvement will be with me for the rest of my life.

"When we walked into the community hall in 2002, it was like walking into a musical instrument."
Mark Finser

Remembering
Steven Moore

April 21, 1939 – March 28, 2004

Carla Beebe Comey

If one were fortunate enough to have had the privilege of knowing Steven Moore in the last years of his life, one would have encountered a wise, humble man of carefully considered words and eye-twinkling humor. As a colleague and teacher, he had the utmost reverence for individual freedom; he listened for questions, answering them with humility and respect. When Steven spoke in a faculty meeting, all listened intently for he did so rarely and when he did, he spoke with profound wisdom.

Solemn as he may have been at times, he was a frequent and energetic onlooker at the local high school basketball games. On field days at the Waldorf school, he played a dramatic game of baseball – to the delight of the students! In the classroom, he was known to collapse backwards when his class would finally meet his expectations. Admired and loved by his students, when the artistic presentations given at the fifth grade Pentathlon in Boulder, Colorado in May of 2004 were dedicated to him, students were excited to raise their hands to indicate they had known him.

A Nebraska native interested in sports, Steven – known then as Rodney – was also bright and somewhat bookish and was sometimes strong-armed into doing his classmates' homework. He graduated from high school as salutatorian and received a full naval scholarship to the University of Nebraska to study engineering and science. In the midst of this course of study, one perhaps chosen by his parents, he was advised by a school psychiatrist to leave the program. After stretches at California colleges, he went to McGill University in Montreal. By then, Steven had shifted his focus of study to the arts, connected with a spiritual teacher, and changed his name to Steven, a move that confused his mother. It was in Montreal that he encountered the works of Rudolf Steiner.

After graduation, Steven made his way to Denver, where he found himself part of the Beat Poet movement. He met a woman who was opening an avant-garde coffeehouse downtown, Merlyn Querido. After eight years and many conversations with Merlyn, he made his way to Emerson College in England to join the Waldorf teacher training course, studying in the speech and eurythmy schools. He completed both courses of study, learned to speak German, and toured with a performing eurythmy troupe throughout the world.

At the end of his world tours, Steven decided to teach eurythmy in Helsinki, Finland – and to learn Finnish, a remarkable feat for an American. He also worked on a touring eurythmy production of the *Kalevala* before returning to the Denver Waldorf School as a eurythmy teacher. After a spell in Australia where he successfully staged a drama he had written, he moved to Paonia, Colorado to recover his health and help create a biodynamic farm at the Lamborn Valley School. His love of drama flourished and he worked closely with Konnelle Stone, Ted Pugh and others to deepen his relationship to this art.

Steven and Holly join the seventh/eighth grade cast members after a performance of **Midsummer Night's Dream**, *May 2001.*

And Steven continued to teach. He lived in a humble cabin in Paonia and taught in the small Lamborn Valley School. In 1993, he responded to a new initiative and made the two-hour trip weekly to teach eurythmy, speech and drama in the Aspen Waldorf School. He helped to hold the spiritual being of this young initiative through its move to Carbondale. The euchre game in which he won a larger eurythmy room has become legendary. He continued to teach in Carbondale and Paonia until he crossed the threshold.

At the time of his passing, the fifth grade at the Waldorf School on the Roaring Fork was in the midst of a production of *Perseus and Andromeda* that Steven had begun with them; it was performed the day after his funeral. The children felt his presence and, remembering his sense of humor, remarked that he had probably caused that day a small glitch in the production. We continue to feel his presence on the stage in our school and are grateful for the wisdom and humor he shared with us.

Remembering
Steven Moore

April 21, 1939 – March 28, 2004

Konnelle Stone

"He taught well because of the way he was able to love people."

Most of the community knew Steven as a teacher, but as his acting and directing teacher, I knew him as an artistic partner and student. Steven developed into a good drama teacher, yes, but not for the reasons you think: He taught well because of the way he was able to love people.

I never saw any human form more beautiful and expressive than Steven's when he performed eurythmy, but he had growing pains as an actor which required constant practice and perseverance. After drinking in all he could in acting classes and rehearsals, he applied the work with discipline, determination and gratitude – and finally, he soared. What he was able to do after his breakthrough truly rivaled the work of an Ian McKellen or a Laurence Olivier. Steven shined with the gifts that cannot be taught: He was a student of life. I wish we all could have seen more of Steven the actor.

Steven took all of the gifts God gave him and used them well, and as in the parable of the talents, they multiplied in the world. He saw the good in people and instilled them with confidence. He knew and loved each of his students in a very personal and specific way. He was comforting and wise and had a tremendous sense of humor. He was a person in whom it was hard to find any faults. He was a writer, poet, teacher, performer, director, scientist, mentor, student and servant. "Well done, thou good and faithful servant: thou hast been faithful over a few things, I will make thee ruler over many things."

Colonel Freeleigh, Steven's character in *Dandelion Summer*, said words Steven might have said: "They sat quietly and listened. And I told them things they never heard… It was worth it. I don't care. I was in a pure fever and I was alive. It doesn't matter if being so alive kills a man; it's better to have the quick fever every time."

"Steven's sudden passing changed the direction that many of us thought we would travel."

Valerie Lee

In 2002, the eighth grade class play was *High Tor*, a sophisticated drama. Steven had chosen this play because *A Midsummer Night's Dream* had been done as a curriculum play the year before with the combined seventh/eighth class. Halfway through play practice he came to me exhausted with the weight of it and said, "Valerie, what can we do with music to lighten this play?" I suggested a sort of Greek chorus singing "Little Rock of Tor" to the title tune from *Little Shop of Horrors*.

Steven tried to take this in, tentatively saying, "Yes, you may have an idea…". What he didn't know was that he was to be part of the chorus which would cross the stage doing the pony and singing!

Finally convinced to try it himself, Steven had to convince the class. I will never forget those long, graceful, spider-like legs coming down the aisle, attempting the pony with the whole class rolling on the floor, laughing. Steven had to sit down and fan himself. We did it, of course, and it worked. It was another statement of Steven's total openness and willingness to allow creative muses to work.

Steven, Konnelle Stone, Summer Cole, Doug Sheffer and I, with Isabelle DeLise on the fringe as a child actress, were moving forward with a small theater ensemble. Steven's sudden passing changed the direction that many of us thought we would travel. My own direction is still being unveiled.

Merlyn Querido

It was I who first suggested to Steven that he teach in Aspen. Although he had been at the Shining Mountain Waldorf School in Boulder, written and produced class plays and taught eurythmy, he had left the school and was living in Paonia. Not everyone understands that social activity weaves a "mantle of warmth" around a school and that schools need eurythmy, drama, speech and music to thrive. Steven brought this through his wonderful teaching. He had endless good will towards people and like René was a shining example of the power of positivity.

"He had endless good will toward people, and was a shining example of the power of positivity."

Remembering
Steven Moore

April 21, 1939 – March 28, 2004

Doug Sheffer

When I think of Steven Moore I think of deliberate grace, of the purposeful life of a person who moved through space like a deer or the wind. There was intention to everything that Steven did. He studied and pondered and planned most of his adult life. He also left a certain amount of room for the unexpected and could be spontaneously funny. He had a wit and a bit of an imp about him. It certainly came out in the verses of his plays, naming giants Snotgard and putting words in stanzas, which simply made the children chuckle.

He loved children and people in general. He could be a "grandfather" to a close friend's child, a "brother" to a parent, an "uncle" to a student in their late teens and a "father" to the child in us all. People sought him out for his advice, which he was usually slow to give, waiting until he had thoroughly considered the question before talking.

Steven was a complex man with many interests, yet simple in his approach to life. He lived simply, he was simply committed to Waldorf education, he dressed simply and ate simple, healthy foods. He loved to follow politics, sports, astronomy, science and technology. He was both of modern times and a bygone era.

He led by example and everyone around him learned. He encouraged people to do or be their best and people grew from association with him. He had a skeptic's approach to a positive outlook on life. Things were going to get better, grow and improve, but only with hard work. Like a gardener, he knew that without constant vigilance the weeds would quickly return.

I miss Steven very, very much. There is not a week that goes by when I am not reminded of him in something I see, hear or read. Steven's not gone; he has just gone on ahead. We will certainly all be there someday. Fair winds, sweet Prince.

"Deliberate grace with a dash of impishness."

Thesa Kallinicos

I met Steven, a tall, thin, young American at Emerson College, England, in 1968. Needing college funds, Steven sold me his Gibson guitar, a smooth sounding instrument that lent encouragement to a beginner. That guitar traveled back to the United States and Steven saw it in my hands when we met again in Paonia in the early 80's. I don't know how Steven arrived there or how he found the Lamborn Valley School, but he was led there and lived there, in a little cabin across the street from the school, until the day he died. He joined our Waldorf school faculty as a mentor, guided our teacher's meetings and wrote plays. He coached us in eurythmy and speech and studied anthroposophy with us. I think it is fair to say he raised the cultural atmosphere of Lamborn Valley and later, the Roaring Fork Valley.

"Here was a man who worked for the betterment of schools until he was worn thin and yet he was unable to retire."

Steven always needed money to live on although he could live on very little because he was the thriftiest person I've known. Yet, he was generous, an artist without a patron. After every conversation, I had the nagging feeling that he needed to ask something of me but during his lifetime, it never occurred to me to ask what. Here was a man who worked for the betterment of many schools until he was worn thin and yet he was unable to retire. Only after his death, clearly and too late, the question came: "Brother, what ails thee?" I treasure the memory of his light heart and enormous talent.

Lora Davis

*Author of **Hiking Trails in the Collegiate Peaks Wilderness Area** and **Wyoming Continental Divide Trail***

Steven came to Paonia seven years after his colleague from Emerson College, Thesa Kallinicos, founded the Lamborn Valley School, officially a Waldorf school for only one year. After Thesa left, Steven stayed and started a small theater group with Konnell Stone, but finding the Aspen Waldorf School was really a lifesaver for him. He hungered for anthroposophy and despite the difficult commute, it reconnected him with his real love.

I was his respite from work. As a boy, he'd hiked and fished with his father and brother in the Snowy Range of Wyoming and he loved the outdoors. I took him hiking and camping in special places I knew about in Colorado and Wyoming.

Adam Stopek's class in costume with Steven Moore after the Michaelmas Celebration

Although his thin body on the hard, cold ground was, well, hard, he was always a good sport. He once tried to teach me to fly-fish but when I reeled in my first fish, it looked so frightened I couldn't stand it and he had to toss it back. He was such a gentle soul I think he never really enjoyed fly-fishing afterwards.

Steven was special to so many people because he really listened to each of us and could offer solutions to complex interpersonal tangles. I was always astounded and would say, "How do you do that?" but I knew it didn't come easily. He devoted real concentration and meditation to the problems we brought to him and that's how he found the solutions.

"He devoted real concentration and meditation to the problems we brought to him and that's how he found the solutions."

One of my fondest and saddest memories was of Steven Moore's memorial at the school. I was overpowered by the depth of love and appreciation for Steven expressed that day. The Waldorf School on the Roaring Fork was the only school he was able to commit to for the long term. His passion for drama and eurythmy was met there, and he was able to create something with the children that was extraordinary. When I saw the portraits of his eurythmy performance there, the spiritual strength and power that exudes from them is an unequivocal statement that he stands as a guardian of this place.

Nancy Blanning

Eurythmy: A New Art of Movement

By Carla Beebe Comey

The word, eurythmy, comes from the Greek, and means beautiful, rhythmic or harmonious movement, but the art form had its beginnings in Germany in 1912 through a collaboration between Rudolf Steiner and Lory Meyer Smits. An oft-published scientific, literary and philosophical scholar, Dr. Steiner was sought out by those seeking a new direction in their chosen fields. Thus it was not surprising that the mother of a young girl would ask him for advice in finding a healing and strengthening form of movement. She was seeking an alternative to ballet and gymnastics for her daughter because she viewed both as hardening.

Steiner began sessions with the 17-year-old Lory Meyer Smits by stating that this new art of movement would first have to do with the spoken word. He told her that it is in speaking that the human be-

ing creates something purely out of himself. His whole being is involved in the gesture behind the speech, but as it comes out in audible form, the whole movement is concentrated into the speech organs and comes out on a stream of air. This out-coming stream takes the exact forms of the words. The two began to explore how to translate the movement that is concentrated into the speech organs into gestures or movements that could be "spoken" with the arms and body. This exploration would become known as speech eurythmy. Steiner and Smits also explored gestures that would be "sung" movement, as opposed to tones being played on a musical instrument. This would become known as tone eurythmy. In both cases, the human body would become the instrument to express, or make visible, the spoken word or musical sounds.

Although eurythmy is first and foremost a performing art, students in the earliest Waldorf schools were given classes in eurythmy. This healing and strengthening form of movement was seen as a necessary part of educating the whole child and it continues to be central to the curriculum. The material for the eurythmy lessons accompanies the other lessons in content; stories, poems and music appropriate to the curriculum are used.

From pre-school through grade three, the children imitate the eurythmy teacher as stories, poems and legends are recited and music is played on various instruments. Gestures and increasingly complex group choreography are introduced solely through imitation. The focus is on moving harmoniously with one another and moving gracefully as an individual. The circle is the primary form in which the students and teacher work together, but a journey through a dark wood may be walked on a large spiral pattern. Crossing a narrow bridge may call for walking a very straight line.

As the children enter fourth grade and continue into fifth grade, the exercises and forms increase in complexity. In addition, students of this age are ready to move as individuals. Eurythmy exercises are introduced in which it is necessary to have a firm grasp on one's own movement while others move differently. These concentration exercises may involve clapping and stepping in changing sequences of spoken numbers or musical rhythms. Precision, harmony and grace are called for. The students also begin to move facing the front of the room, following patterns drawn on the board, as individuals or groups with different parts. In addition, the students become conscious of the gestures they have been making for several years. The lesson in which each student's name is gestured in eurythmy is often full of excitement and wonder as they discover how well they already know the secret eurythmy language.

In the middle school years, the group forms become more challenging, as do the individual exercises. The children not only move another form or part against others, but they are asked to do two or three different things themselves. An example would be to walk the bass line of a piece of music and at the same time clap the rhythm of the notes of the melody. The students of grades six, seven and eight also enjoy returning to the material of the earlier eurythmy lessons to create performances for the younger students, designing the choreography and gestures themselves.

Humor is essential to the middle school lessons and gestures with the feet and head often provide humorous additions to these stories and poems.

As part of the Waldorf curriculum, eurythmy provides the student with an opportunity to learn coordination, spatial awareness, concentration, self-awareness, presence of mind, active listening and an ability to move harmoniously with others. Students learn these skills through movement that arises out of the human being, movement that has been seen as healing and strengthening.

Valerie Lee

When Valerie joined us, the school began to ring out with music.

My beginning with the Waldorf school came when I began looking for a preschool for my son, Sam, in 1995. In the Yellow Brick School, on a sweet little table, was a brochure. I was astounded by what I read and wondered where I had been to have missed Waldorf education, Steiner, and all of this.

I spoke to Kathryn King, sitting on a couch in her small office, and as I listened to snippets about music and Waldorf education, I was pulled back to my own childhood. She talked about weaving the music into the curriculum, something I had longed for as a child when, for me, everything was a song. On our Wyoming ranch, my sister and I did the dishes together and we would have to run into the living room, stand on the hearth, and sing and dance for Mom and Dad. Finally our mother had to separate us because the dishes were not getting done!

I was deeply impressed with the freedom of the education, the openness and at the same time, the groundedness. It wasn't just an alternative. There were answers as to why we educated differently. My intellect was captivated when I heard, "We don't do minor mode until the child is ready to look inside, old enough to be contemplative." What deep logic!

In the fall of 1995, I began spending my lunch hours as the eurythmy accompanist for Steven Moore. He became my mentor: in the curriculum, in anthroposophy, and as a developing human being. He opened many doors on my journey. I returned to piano and remembered the love I had had for composition and improvisation.

My first collaboration on plays was *Perseus and Andromeda*, performed by Patty Fox's fifth grade at Paepcke Auditorium. I took the assignment very seriously thinking, "How am I to find ancient Greek music? There is very little written down." Fortunately Kathryn had a few one-line Greek melodies and I wrote the rest. By the time of the performance, the orchestra – Julie Paxton and I – sat surrounded by xylophones, flutes and some lyres that I didn't know how to play – and made ancient Greek music! Later Steven would just say, "We need some water music. Traveling music. Music to go up the hill by." And it would come. I realized that I wasn't writing the music. It was the children writing it – through me.

On Mother's Day in 1996, Patty Fox asked if I would "mother" the music program at the school. I said, "Yes! I want the job!" and then remembered I already had a job – which I resigned the next day. I had no Waldorf training but was being trained unofficially by Steven and Kathryn. When I attended my first conference at Rudolf Steiner College, I was introduced to the Werbeck voice method and heard Dennis Klocek speak. Afterwards Kathryn asked me to write about Dennis' talk and I said, "I'm not going to be able to do that." It was so familiar and yet so foreign, like learning a new language that you can intuitively understand but when you try to speak, you have no vocabulary. I couldn't wait to hear more.

In my interview I was asked what I could bring, besides music, to the school. I said I could expose the school in the community because I was well known. At Christmas, we were ready to perform and brought the whole school of twenty-eight children in borrowed white robes with red and green collars to sing at the Sardy House tree-lighting.

We sang in four languages and everyone wanted to know who we were, where we came from. The children were young, still with high voices and it was beautiful to start working with their breath through the flutes and then taking that breath into the singing voice. I set up a formula for concerts that I've repeated since: classical, world music and American music. After Christmas, our first orchestra, Patty's class of nine girls and one boy, began practicing all stacked up in a tiny room. In the spring, we held a memorable concert with choir and orchestra in the Aspen Chapel.

That spring and summer we built the school in Carbondale but the fall brought a big change for me when Sam had his first seizure. I took a sabbatical through 1998 but came back in January of 1999, volunteering to collaborate with Steven in providing the music for class plays. In the fall of 1999, I was employed to provide a fulltime program as eurythmy accompanist, orchestra and choir teacher, and drama collaborator. That spring we held our second big spring concert, in part because I wanted the community to feel how desperately we needed the new community hall. And feel it they did! Each grade, one through eight, performed several songs and one dance – from Broadway hits to Celtic jigs. We did orchestra, we did brass, we did adult choir. Parents were hanging from the ceiling to see their children. The community hall was guaranteed!

By the end of 2000 I found I couldn't manage a fulltime job and Sam too. But when the school decided not to replace me, I recommitted to teach music in the lower grades and raise $10,000 through grants and private donations to fund the upper grades' instrumental program. I resigned again in 2003 to join Steven and Konnelle as music director of the theater ensemble project. I loved my time at the Waldorf School on the Roaring Fork and still miss the children and the music we made together.

Music in the Waldorf Curriculum

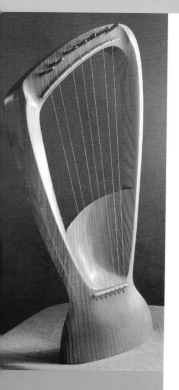

by Andrea Lyman

Certified Waldorf music teacher, mentor and president of the Association of North American Waldorf Music Educators (ANAWME)

Music is an art that allows each child to experience what it is to be fully human. It harmonizes with the child's own innate musicality, which is a reflection of the music of the entire cosmos. Music in the Waldorf curriculum awakens and nurtures this deep inner life of the child. Like the main lesson curriculum, the music curriculum follows very specific stages of development. The study and experience of the various elements in music engage the thinking, feeling and willing in every child. A strong music curriculum can develop and nurture the very forces necessary to be able to meet the challenges of the world with enthusiasm and confidence.

In grade one, singing freely in the "mood of the fifth" permeates the music classes. The young child resonates naturally with this floating, 'unfinished' quality in music. A variety of instrumental sounds are used for tone color and mood to accompany singing or playing. Attention is given to the in- and out-breath using flowing silks during singing and playing, as well as to some work with children's lyre, but no orchestral instruments.

In grade two, music continues to be presented in an imaginative way through the mood and feeling life of the child. The music curriculum attends to polarities and contrasts in music: listening versus making music, and dualities in the musical elements (high and low, loud and soft, fast and slow, differences in tone colors, etc.). Formal musical terms come later but the feeling or mood of such qualities is experienced by the children.

During grade three, a transformation occurs, often referred to as the nine-year change. The psychological development of the children at this time makes it possible to introduce traditional musical notation. Just as, historically, the first notation was used for sacred songs, so the children begin singing the major scale with the main emphasis in the repertoire being the sacred element in song. The condition of the human being, standing between the spiritual and the earthly, is a balance that is in question during the nine-year change. Sacred music is one way for humans to explore this condition.

The Choroi diatonic flute is also introduced and the children learn the C major scale. Folk songs, a more earthly expression, provide material for flute work. The musical element of beat is introduced and simple percussion instruments are used to explore beat and rhythm. Every student begins the violin and plays it throughout the year.

In connection with fractions, introduced in fourth grade, the children learn to listen to and write notes of different lengths and sense intervals. By the end of grade four, all the children should be able to sight-read simple melodies on their instruments as well as vocally. Rounds are introduced, including easier canons, descants and quodlibets (partner songs).

The golden age of childhood, fifth grade, is the fulcrum point of the grade school years and a new need for harmony exists. An overriding theme of this year is the magnificent and inspirational Greek mood. Like the Greek ideal, the songs should embody grace, beauty and balance. Folk ballads and American folk songs and dances are used to practice songs with harmonic accompaniments in alternating listening and singing.

In grade six, the study of the Middle Ages permeates the music curriculum and there is a vast repertoire for this time period. The children's voices are

Patty Fox's combined sixth/seventh grade, Mayfaire, 1998

The music explored attempts to meet this deeply stirring, often disturbing, always inward, quality. Theory, composition and more complex part-singing are continued. Ensemble work is paramount and the ensembles can provide music for school festivals throughout the year.

Music in the Waldorf curriculum seeks to nourish and strengthen the living, healing presence of music in the life of the developing human being and provides an opportunity to experience both one's individuality and relationship to community.

still pure and unchanged for the most part, and singing plain chant (known as Gregorian chant) is perfect for the sixth grader. Elements of the medieval vocal style and instruments and traditional wooden recorders in all voices (soprano, alto, tenor and bass) are studied using this music.

Grade seven is flavored by the Renaissance, the Age of Exploration and Discovery in geography, science, astronomy and many other areas. Both vocal and instrumental music of the Renaissance is presented during this time. Recorders are used extensively as they are classic instruments of the Renaissance.

The eighth grade year is a year of struggles, freedoms and ideals – the revolutions. This is also the end of a seven-year cycle and the beginning of the new perspective of adolescence.

*Above: Valerie Lee assembled the first adult choir to sing at Mayfaire in 1996. It has continued to grow and now performs at school celebrations and in the Roaring Fork community as **The Waldorf Revelers**.*

Right: Rhianna Borderick and Alexander Erdman

Lorraine Curry

Lorraine has been making music at the school for seven years.

I was hired by Robin Marcus to teach strings for her fifth/sixth grade in 1999. After my first day, I remember that I went home with my cheeks hurting from smiling so much. Everyone was so sweet! There were so many parents giving their time. If I had known of Waldorf ten years earlier, I would have gone for the training and become a class teacher.

After Robin left, Frau Hauk, started helping me to understand the curriculum. She also advised me to stop wearing so much black. As a musician, it was practically all that I had in my closet. Eventually I learned from Priscilla Dickinson that there are colors specific to each day of the week and that when teaching in the lower grades it is best to wear lighter colors. Steven Moore and Hartmut Schiffer began answering my growing questions about anthroposophy. Valerie Lee has been my musical mentor, always having her fingers on the pulse of music education in the Waldorf movement.

Adam Stopeck taught me about the third grade curriculum and I wrote a series of violin pieces that would go with Old Testament stories. I used Suzuki methods that added a new technique to each piece so the children could grow musically.

I feel extremely fortunate to be able to teach strings in a beautiful school, where music is so well supported and encouraged. At times, a specialty teacher might feel like a satellite to the rest of the faculty. My advice is to ask questions; the answers you hear will astonish you and promote deeper questions.

Helena Hurrell

The Spirit of the School reaffirms the ever-present help of the Spiritual Worlds.

I was drawn to the Carbondale school as if in a dream. In fact, it was a dream. In late November of 1997, when I was living in Boulder, Colorado I felt inspired to visit my niece in Basalt. The first night after I arrived, I had a dream in which a friend appeared to me and told me that it was time for me to resume my destiny as a Waldorf teacher and that I was going to move to Carbondale and join the Waldorf school there.

My first encounter with Waldorf education had been 20 years earlier in a San Francisco coffee shop that was owned by a woman from Germany who had been involved with Rudolf Steiner's work for many years. I was looking at the art on the wall of the café; it was a series of paintings by the children of the San Francisco Waldorf School. There was something about the quality of the colors, which deeply affected me. I later learned of the training schools and went to Fair Oaks, California where I was fortunate to live with the Queridos, founders of Rudolf Steiner College. While I was there I completed a foundation year in Anthroposophy. I then moved to England for a year's study in Anthroposophical Art Therapy. While there I met Margret Meyerkort and completed a years course in Waldorf Early Childhood Education. From there my journey took me to Australia, Boulder and Carbondale, Colorado, and now California. My great aunt, Beulah Emmet, founded the High Mowing Waldorf School in New Hampshire.

After awakening from my dream, I telephoned the school and left a message. Kathryn King, the school's development director, returned the call a short while later. She asked me to come visit and possibly interview for a job. I came along with my significant other/husband Edward and sat with Kathryn, Barbi Sheffer, Frances Lewis and Julie McCallan. I was most impressed by the Roaring Fork School because they also asked questions of Edward, as to how a possible move would affect him. There was a warmth in the environment that you could feel. I immediately noticed how the faculty and parents were deeply engaged in the life of the school. They had just finished the first building.

Three months later in February 1998, Edward, our three boys and I moved to Carbondale and my sixteen-month relationship with the school began. The kindergarten was in what is now the first grade as none of the other buildings had been built yet. It was a wonderful time for us. As quickly as we came, however, we were catapulted away. Lewis, my middle son, was in need of serious medical attention. The insurance company dictated that if surgery was to be performed, it had to be in California. So, at a moment's notice in June 1999, off to California we went.

Recently, my connection with the Roaring Fork kindergarten has been renewed. I have returned to the school on several occasions to lead the Nurturing Arts Workshop and mentor the teachers. Each time I'm here, I feel that I encounter the uplifting quality of the school's spiritual strivings and the presence of people like Steven Moore, who gave so much of themselves to nurture this special place.

Chapter 7

Millennial School

We passed through the challenges of the nine-year change as the millennium approached. Some feared a world-wide technological collapse, others hoped for a new beginning of peace and prosperity. When our advisor, Eugene Schwartz, published *The Millennial Child,* some looked to it for insights into our millennial school.

In an historical review of educational methods and underlying philosophical ethos covering a decade, a century, even a millennium, Eugene identifies cyclical patterns. In the first third of the time period, the head (thinking) predominates. In the central third, the heart (feeling) is most active. The hands (doing) dominate in the last third of the time period.

"I will approach the course of the century as the unfolding of human consciousness which is manifested in three discrete stages. What appears first is an idea, a thought-form, worked out and expressed in the first third of the century. The idea is gradually taken up by the next generation, and whether it is accepted or rejected, it nonetheless is imbued with a new component as it is taken into the life of feelings and emotions. Finally in the last third of the century, the first generation's ideas, imbued with the second generation's feelings, are acted upon, and become an impulse of will for the century's last generation. Hence, the task of Generation One is to develop the element of thinking, the work of Generation Two is to embody those thoughts with feeling, and the activity of Generation Three is to act on those thoughts and feelings out of the depths of its willing. The achievements of Generation Three will in turn be "grist for the mill," the foundation for the thinkers of the twenty-first century's Generation One" (p 6).

Now a "millennial school" filled with its share of "millennial children," the Waldorf School on the Roaring Fork recognized that major structural and governance changes would be necessary to meet the demands of the new century. Although it is common for the founding parents of a school to withdraw once the school has turned nine, many of our original families were still deeply involved. This made for a continuity of consciousness and commitment that could serve as a strong and will-imbued foundation for the school's next step.

In 2000, Patty Fox, founder and lead teacher, graduated the second half of her class and retired. Bill Fordham, Dana's husband and Patty's longtime friend returned to the Roaring Fork school from the original Waldorf school in Stuttgart, where he had been teaching English as a second language since Dana's death. Deeply schooled in anthroposophy and school governance, and a master teacher, Bill's enthusiasm synchronized with the current of change that was already being generated by parents and teachers. Bringing fresh thought to the new millennium, Bill saw immediately that an organ unique to this time and this school, coupled with deep study, was needed to take the school to its next level. He went to work and faculty, board of trustees and parent council worked with him.

Bill envisioned a community council that would be a central organ able to both lead and modulate the three other bodies. It would become a "first response" unit and would also address continuing personnel questions in a timely manner. It would organize and prioritize the issues facing the school so that each body would operate more effectively.

Even as these innovative and exciting changes were taking place on the level of governance, the school's rapid expansion made demands of often heroic proportions that teachers and parents struggled to meet. Bill Fordham became ill and resigned in his second year. Adam Stopeck, who had taken a class from first into fifth grade, had to resign at the year's end. Holly Richardson graduated her two eighth grades and offered to help Frances Lewis divide her seventh and eighth grade, but when Holly's pregnancy demanded bed rest, adjustments had to be made again. Lyman Jackson came from Denver to fill Holly's space. Kate Friesen agreed to fill the vacancy left by the departure of Richard Weiss.

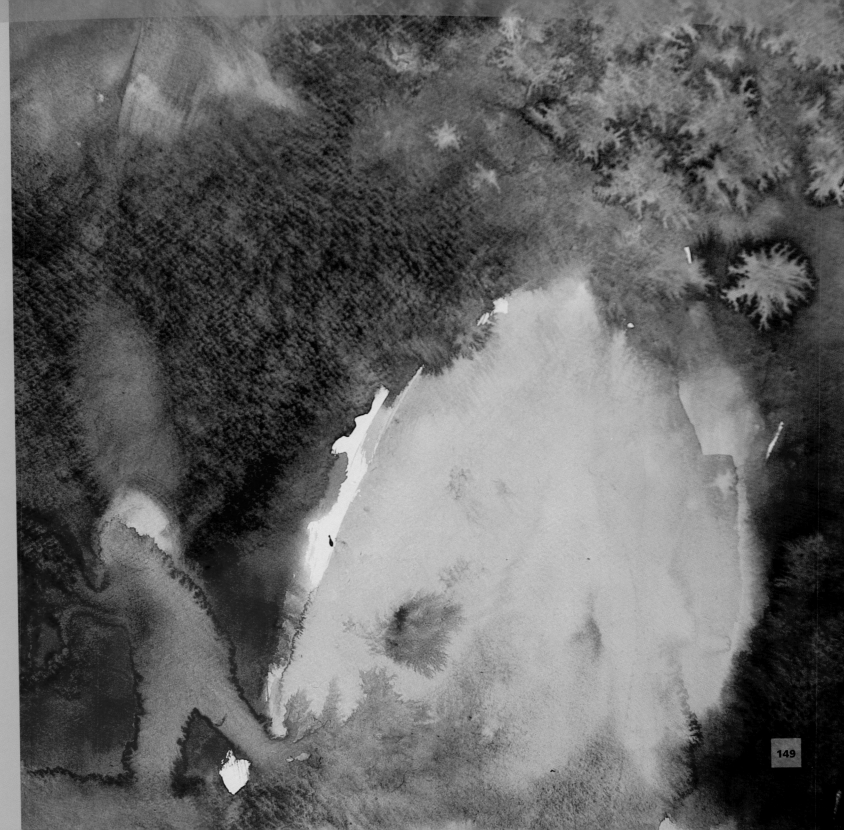

As parents, teachers, and staff rose again and again to meet the challenges of running a viable school in the new millennium, the Waldorf School on the Roaring Fork moved forward with renewed clarity. The opening of the new community hall in 2002 made manifest the central role of community building in the life of the school.

Bill Fordham

Dana and Bill Fordham were inspirational in the school's early years. Later, Bill helped start the community council and the mentoring support team.

I first heard of the Aspen initiative in 1991 when Patty Fox and Betsy Engelman came to the Denver Waldorf School to meet my wife, Dana, who had offered to teach kindergarten in their summer camp at Windstar. Dana and I had met when we taught together at the Rudolf Steiner School in New York City and we had been teaching in Waldorf schools here and in Germany for ten years.

There was an instant connection between Dana and the Aspen initiative. She shepherded their camp and their first year. The next summer, we brought our two boys and we both taught the camp, a very special and memorable time. But it was at the end of that summer that we learned Dana had cancer. The more I think about my connection to the Aspen school, the more I keep coming back to Dana. The school is more about her than it is me and the boys. Aspen, Windstar and the people were for her Paradise on Earth, the place she needed to discover on earth in order to cross over.

She left us in August of 1993 and we scattered her ashes at Windstar. I continued to teach in the Denver Waldorf School, and then returned to the Stuttgart (Germany) Waldorf School. When I came back to Colorado to visit in 2000, I was invited to join the Waldorf School on the Roaring Fork. I continue to believe that somehow Dana knew that only near her, through her, in and around her and her friends, could I confront myself and my illness. I taught the first-grade class there in 2000 but my personal struggles escalated, at which time, I left the school. After spending almost a year away from teaching, I accepted the challenging task of teaching a seventh grade in an inner-city Waldorf school. Once that year ended, I privately studied speech formation in Spring Valley before moving to Nairobi, Kenya in the summer of 2005 to help with a Waldorf initiative there. I have found it to be much like WSRF in its community involvement. Although here the beauty is surrounded with high-security fencing, the people are longing to rediscover community in a world polarized and dominated by nationalist interests.

Despite my short tenure at the Waldorf School on the Roaring Fork, I found there was work I could do to help develop the administrative bodies of the school in a way that better mirrored this community, this campus. When Rudolf Steiner first gave the indications for schools to be administered by experienced faculty through the College of Teachers, the Waldorf impulse was very young. Now we have crossed into a new millennium and a new cultural epoch in which our work within the community is not only with children, but also with parents. It is perhaps our most important work. Finding healthy forms for that work is a new quest for Waldorf schools.

When I arrived, the school was just emerging from a period when relationships were strained between the parents and faculty. Yet there was a tremendously involved and sincere community of parents, teachers and board members who wanted to strengthen the school. To do this, I felt they needed to learn to work meditatively in a new structure that included representatives from all three bodies. At our annual Janus meeting in 2000, I proposed the formation of the community council.

In the beginning, there were seven members of the council: three teachers, including the faculty chairperson, the president of the parent council and another council member, the board president and the school administrator. A four-person subcommittee of the council also met once a week to review issues and correspondence, prepare the agenda for its weekly meeting, and distribute tasks to the other

bodies of faculty, parent council and board of trustees. The community council became a sort of "ego" for the school while the faculty was the "heart" that ensouled the education. This left the faculty more time for pedagogical study and for developing forms for evaluation, self-evaluation and observation. The mentoring support team became a sort of college of teachers, in that they were the more experienced faculty members who were also willing to provide a liaison between teachers and parents with concerns.

Once the community council began operating, decisions were more easily processed, the study of anthroposophy was enhanced and communications were eased. A body had formed itself of individuals making decisions for individuality. The Steiner verse that guided this endeavor began our meetings:

The healthy social life is found
When in the mirror of each human soul
The whole community finds its reflection
And when in the community
The virtue of each one is living.

Since that time, other Waldorf schools have taken an interest in the community council structure as a model for their schools. I believe it reflects the communities that grow up around Waldorf schools today. Parents want to be involved; they want to be empowered. School faculties need the broad view of their communities that can only be understood when parents and board members have an equal voice with teachers. The community council certainly mirrors the WSRF campus in which the community hall is the gathering place, the center for the school.

Adam Stopeck

Adam met and married Patty Doyle – and Waldorf education – when the school was young. He now teaches at the Sunrise Waldorf School in Canada.

I taught at the Waldorf School on the Roaring Fork for four and a half years, from fall of 1999 to December of 2003. I took a class of well-prepared children from the kindergarten of Helena Hurrell and had great hopes for our journey together when I told the children my first fairy tale at the Rose Ceremony on a clear fall day. The highlight of the first year was the performance of the play *The Two Brothers*, a Grimm's fairy tale that my wife, Patty, and I collaborated on.

From second grade on I had the great good fortune to work with Bill Fordham. Bill was a highly experienced Waldorf class teacher and foreign language teacher who had had a relationship with our school from the beginning. He came to us from seven years at the Stuttgart Waldorf School to teach our first grade and German. Watching Bill teach German to my class gave me great inspiration as a teacher. Fourth grade was particularly rewarding as the children and I greatly enjoyed the Norse stories. I still look back with joy on the last day of school that year when we performed *The Colorado Trail*. It was truly a multidisciplinary work of singing, drama, dancing, recorder playing and drumming. For fourth graders to accomplish this made me very proud.

The curriculum of fifth grade was again deeply satisfying. I felt the class was coming together in many respects as we were doing some of our best work in all areas of school life. Regretfully, this analysis was not shared by all in the school community and my relationship with the school ended abruptly.

"Eugene Schwartz said in a lecture, 'Waldorf is a revolutionary teaching method.' I was enrolled at Rudolf Steiner College a week later."

Right: Emma Braddy, Maddalena Deorsola, Rosie Mertz, Taila Maat, Tessa Ebert

Mathematics in the Waldorf School

As distilled from Eugene Schwartz's description at www.millennialchild.com

Mathematics, more than any other subject in the Waldorf school, supports both the child's inner development and the historical unfolding of the curriculum. Mathematical truths are self-evident: evident to the child's lively senses in the primary grades and evident to the adolescent's awakening intellect in the upper grades. Arithmetic and later mathematics are "age specific" because number concepts are closely connected to the mental and physical development of the growing human being. For example, the growth spurt in the bones of the arms and hands at age ten lays a foundation for the study for fourth grade arithmetic. The single humerus of the upper arm meets the two bones (ulna and radius) of the lower arm, which in turn "divide" into two rows of four carpals each – a wonderful basis on which to build the teaching

of fractions. In adolescence, however, the orderly and harmonious growth processes of earlier childhood are disturbed. Scores of new chemicals are secreted by the body's glandular system, and neither physiological nor emotional balance is easily attained by the teenager. With this in mind, it is not difficult to understand why the lawful and inexorable balance of the linear equation can be so satisfying for the seventh grader studying algebra.

Children come to first grade counting. The combination of rhythm and change is very harmonizing and is practiced to one hundred – and back! Counting rhythms are then varied by speaking some numbers loudly and others quietly – and the times tables begin to appear. While the times tables will be practiced up to eighth grade and will finally be a rote process, the comfort of stamping, clapping, jumping and shouting the tables and seeing them in beautiful forms gets the numbers into the children's bodies and strengthens them for a lifetime of mathematics.

From counting as a rhythmic activity to counting objects is another challenge for the first grader. "How many?" is powerfully awakening as is the concept of "one" (a cardinal number) – "I have one shell" – versus "first" (an ordinal number) – "I am first!" The qualities of numbers, one through twelve, are brought through the fairy tales (*The Three Little Pigs, The Six Swans, The Seven Ravens*) and other imaginative stories. While numerology has been popularized recently by Dan Brown and others, the ancient study of number qualities has

enriched many a math student's life and offers abundant material to Waldorf teachers throughout the eight years of the lower school.

The exploration of number qualities leads to the four arithmetic operations of addition, subtraction, multiplication and division, again brought through stories. Often the teacher develops gnome-like characters with the temperaments of the phlegmatic (always adding more), the melancholic (always losing something), the sanguine (gathering in multitudes) and the choleric (dividing evenly). These basic processes are strengthened in first through eighth grade through daily exercises: following mental math journeys, working on story problems and playing games. Place value is explored in second grade and extended each year through positive and negative roots and exponents in eighth.

In third grade, measurement is added. The children learn that the ancients measured the earth to build structures and till the land, as they will do as part of the third grade curriculum. To do so, they will learn the complex if "antiquated" system of English measurement: measuring inches, feet and yards with linear measurements based on 12, measuring weight (ounces and pounds) on a base of 16, measuring liquids (cups, pints, quarts, gallons) on a base of 4, and measuring money on a base of 10. Rudolf Steiner praised the American system because it forces us to be flexible – and it certainly challenges the third grader.

As children pass through the nine-year change between third and fourth grade, they separate "self" from "other." It is time to introduce fractions and move from the sensory-based operations of arithmetic to the concepts of mathematics. While it is still possible to understand fractions as "pieces of the pie," it requires a conceptual leap to understand that the greater the denominator, the smaller the fraction. The children will be led from manipulation to concept and back again through the eighth grade when their ability to think abstractly begins to mature. The new concepts of factoring, applying the four operations to fractional numbers, learning about abundant and deficient numbers, magic squares and the sieve of Eratosthenes open a window on future numerical possibilities.

While all of these processes require continued practice, fifth grade is the time to introduce decimals, a special kind of fraction that hearkens back to the measurement of money learned in third grade. Children also apply decimal concepts to the metric system and to freehand geometrical designs based on Greek divisions using the circle and the arc, fractional divisions of the line, and the triangle. A proof of the Pythagorean Theorem caps fifth grade.

As students grow more discerning, geometry in sixth grade externalizes the mechanical nature of the eye and arm with a T-square, straight-edge and compass. Precise geometric constructions divide the circle into squares, pentagons and pentagrams, and hexagons. Further divisions are carefully and artistically colored, creating forms that are often frameable. As geometric forms grow more familiar, the formulas for their area, perimeter and circumference are introduced.

Business math, also studied in sixth grade, supplies practical uses for circle and bar graphs and deepens the understanding of decimals by ap-

plying them to percentage, interest, taxation, profit and loss, markups and markdowns. The history of trade and banking is incorporated into medieval studies and grounds the students in the realities of the financial world. In sixth grade, too, the students often begin raising money for their class trips and careful accounting of their income and expenses adds real experiences to their studies.

Seventh graders study the Renaissance and are ready for their personal "birth of intellectual discovery." Algebra begins with the challenging study of positive and negative numbers, integers which demand both imagination and precise manipulation. The laws of balance that underlie algebraic equations grow out of the extended number line. Practical problems in time and distance, ratio and proportion ground the work in the real world. Exponents, powers and roots are introduced; geometry is further studied with the relationship of angles.

In eighth grade, the Golden Rectangle and the Golden Proportion, phi, (1.618), a ratio which underlies organic growth in plants, animals and

the human being, are explored. The logarithmic spiral which grows out of this proportion and is the mediator between the circle and the straight line may be examined in sunflowers, the chambered nautilus and galaxies; the Fibonacci Series of numbers and its relation to the spiral may be appreciated in pianos and pineapples. The basic axioms, theorems and proofs of Euclidean Geometry will be learned as a basis for logical thinking. These will be extended into Solid Geometry and the Platonic Solids will be molded in clay. Formulas for volume and surface are learned.

In mathematics, ancient number systems with different bases, first introduced with measurement in third grade, will be extended into an appreciation of modern computer science. In algebra, factoring polynomials as a basis for understanding quadratic or "second degree equations" will be undertaken. These equations with two answers meet the polarizing forces experienced by the adolescent and again confirm the age-specific nature of mathematics and its laudable introduction in the Waldorf school curriculum.

Julie Mulcahy

Julie brought six of her seven children to the school, first in California and then Colorado, working tirelessly as a volunteer and then as the enrollment coordinator.

I have great memories of my early Catholic schooling with a community of big families celebrating seasonal and traditional festivals together. I so wanted my children to have the same warm experience. By the time my fourth child, Katy, came along (with three others under 5!), I was looking for the right school. I can't even remember how (It must have been angels!) a group of us came together in a city park and decided to share home-schooling, taking turns teaching the group of ten children. Someone saw what we were doing and asked if we were a Waldorf school.

Kelsea Mulcahy at the Medieval games

We didn't know what a Waldorf school was and someone suggested we go to nearby Rudolf Steiner College in Sacramento to find out. We were immediately enchanted and asked if we could have a teacher. They laughed, "You don't just hire a teacher and have a Waldorf school!" But angels intervened again. Nancy Poer, a founding member of Steiner College, lived close to us and her husband had been in an accident which kept her at home instead of traveling as a Waldorf consultant. She said if we'd fix up her barn and commit to a study group, work on Saturdays and pay tuition, she'd teach our children. Thus began the Cedar Springs Waldorf School, now 160 students strong. Two of those first parents, Patti and Tim Connolly, started their teacher training at RSC the next year and Patti taught at Ceder Springs for 13 years. In 2004 we persuaded them both to come to the Waldorf School on the Roaring Fork as administrator and faculty chair. Small world, Waldorf!

It was hard to leave California but Aspen had a Waldorf school, too, though not a class for Ki, our oldest. Mariah, Kelsea and Katy enrolled. I loved being home with the little ones, so didn't rush to put them into preschool. Our special outings were the days I drove the bus to pick up the "downvalley children." We'd come early to watch the children end their day with verse and happy smiles.

But enrollment in Aspen was a struggle. We planned every event for the public to try to attract more people: class plays, festivals, lectures and workshops. I remember Patty Fox's fifth grade play, *Perseus and Andromeda* in Paepcke Auditorium. It was a big theater but just our families were there with maybe one or two others. By 1996, we were preparing to look for a new home in the mid-valley where more families live year-round and my husband, Michael, and Bob Schultz conducted a long-term planning meeting in the basement of the Yellow Brick that we all attended. Our '96 Mayfaire was in Basalt and then we opened the Children's Garden in Blue Lake and held our Winterfaire and Advent Garden there all on the same day. I was in charge of Winterfaire and it was an all-out effort. We transformed that square white room into a wonderland with blue clouds and snowflakes. At the end of the Advent Garden after the public left, we sang carols together, watching the beeswax candles burn down. It was a very special moment.

In 1998, we moved the school to Carbondale and I cherish the memories of the community building effort, the excitement of moving into our new straw-bale home and the confidence that now the school would grow. And grow it did! Our student population nearly doubled and we added new faculty members. New and old families continued to volunteer, making the campus really special. However, the rapid growth came with challenges, some predictable and some unforeseen. There was the struggle of forming a parent council that blended older school families with families new to the school's philosophy, and there were divisions among faculty members. Only after some time had passed did we come to understand that this struggle was necessary to bring forth the strength and courage needed for the future. My personal life was also under great stress that year, which eventually resulted in a divorce. I wonder now what all of our stars were doing at that time.

With new resolve, I applied to help out in the tiny office of our new school building, not sure if my gifts and mothering experience would fit the needs of the position being offered. But here I've stayed, first as a part-time outreach person, and now as enrollment coordinator. The best part of my job is looking out my office window in this beautiful new community hall building and watching the arrival of the children in the morning, the buzz of parents exchanging ideas, and the engaging creative play on the playground.

We'll soon be enrolled to our maximum capacity and have to look for more land. From its modest beginning in California to our school in Colorado, the experience has been just what I hoped for my children.

Hartmut Schiffer

Hartmut joined the Waldorf School on the Roaring Fork community at a time in his life when most teachers are enjoying retirement.

I first learned of Waldorf education in my home country of Germany. By 1960, at thirty-five, I was ready to move to the United States and begin my teacher training at Highland Hall in Los Angeles. The very next year the training moved to Sacramento, California and so did my family. There, in the 60's, I met many remarkable thinkers and educators. Hermann Von Baravalle was one such person of note. His genius for mathematics guided me through many hours of class preparation in later years.

I started my teaching career with a combined second/third grade class which I taught for four years at which time I took ill and had to stop for a while. It would be my fate as a class teacher to stand before classes which had lost their teacher for one reason or another. All in all, I worked at eight Waldorf schools in the United States and Europe; five as a class teacher and the other three as a subject teacher teaching clay, woodworking, German and English. In 1988 I was able to tie up some loose ends in my life and completed a Masters of Education at Pacific Western University in Los Angeles.

Then came my retirement in 1990, thirty years after I first enrolled in training. That lasted for nine years at which point I ended up in Boulder. There, at the urging of René Querido, I came up to Carbondale to help with the fifth grade. Patty Doyle eventually took that class and I started substituting for Frances Lewis and then for all the grades plus helping in the kindergarten. When Steven Moore was away for his four week break in January, I would lead math lessons in the fifth through eighth grades and do geometric constructions and German tutoring.

Now at age 80, I am happy to be the "grandfather" of the school. I established the teacher library and helped to organize the children's library. I also spend much time in the gardens for instance working to reestablish some balance among the irises and lavender out front of the West Wing. The precocious iris crowd out the humble lavender and need regular thinning.

"Waldorf Education and its underlying anthroposophical truths broadened my knowledge, increased my self-awareness and gave my life direction with the community of man."

The move to Carbondale came at a time in my life when I realized I wanted to dedicate the remainder of my life to Waldorf. Perhaps I will be around long enough to see the woodworking, clay and handwork programs get their own spaces. It is important to dedicate a place where children can come to work with their hands, activities that help develop and strengthen a creative will and harmonize their life forces.

The key to learning and the future of the school is the relationship of the student and the teacher. If the teacher is truly interested in what (s)he is presenting, the children are interested too.

Now the school must consolidate all its programs and parts. Then the quality and reputation of the school will be assured. The WSRF will then be ready for a high school. I also hope that I will be here to see that day arrive.

Narayan Koss and Dawson Struempler

"I have come to understand how critical handwork is to strengthening the child's will and how without it, children lack the sense of creation and self-esteem that is so important today."

Jill Scher

Jill's journey to the Waldorf School began in 1975.

My journey to the Waldorf school began in 1975 when my identical twin sister, Jan, took me to Bavaria to help her cook at a macrobiotic summer camp. She met her husband there and in time they moved to Seattle, began studying anthroposophy, and then completed their teacher training at Rudolf Steiner College. Jan told me it would be easy for me to be a Waldorf teacher because so much of our family life, with seven girls and two boys, was rich in artistic expression. My parents were on a spiritual quest, moving here to study macrobiotics, there to dip into esoteric Christianity, Buddhism or EST. My dad taught himself guitar and we sang all the time, union songs, protests songs, songs about train wrecks and ships sinking. Looking back, we laugh, but now three of my siblings are composers and all of us work with our hands.

While Jan was studying at RSC, I was living a subsistence lifestyle in an isolated part of West Virginia with no phone, just raising my children and weaving. But I missed my family, especially my twin, and in 1985, I visited her in California. She was living a few blocks from the college, with single moms who were also in teacher training. In the afternoons they had tea parties or recorder concerts in their garden. I didn't know what I thought about Waldorf ideas, but what I was feeling was peace and that spoke strongly to me; I wanted to stay.

But I didn't stay. Instead my family moved with me so that I could enroll in the Rhode Island School of Design and our children could enroll in the Meadowbrook Waldorf School. My husband worked in their kindergarten and had a home childcare. I assisted in handwork during our last year there but I still wanted to work as a textile designer, so in 1997 we moved to North Carolina and learned how to be "out in the world," which was good for us. By now, my parents, two sisters and two brothers had settled in the Roaring Fork Valley and, missing my family, I decided to interview for the handwork position at the Waldorf School on the Roaring Fork. It took some time for the position to be resolved but I brought my North Carolina job with me, a wonderful solution financially. I began assisting with handwork in the spring of 2001. The next year, I took over the upper grades and in 2002 taught all of the handwork.

After that year, I knew I needed the Waldorf training, so I started the three-year part-time training for specialty teachers at RSC. It's three weeks in the summer and a week in February. The first week is foundation studies but the next two are a mixed bag of foundation studies and artistic work with handwork-specific classes in the afternoon. We have a dynamic group from all over the world that includes foreign language students who were political refugees and middle-age executives from high-powered careers who want to be high school teachers. We'll stay together all three years and always, I come back inspired.

Despite what Jan said so many years ago about becoming a Waldorf teacher, I'm still finding my way in terms of teaching and classroom management. Sometimes I feel worn and wonder, "Where do I draw the line with discipline? Is this really my work?" However, I have come to understand how critical handwork is to strengthening the child's will and how without it, children lack the sense of creation and self-esteem that is so important today. I'm going to keep working at it.

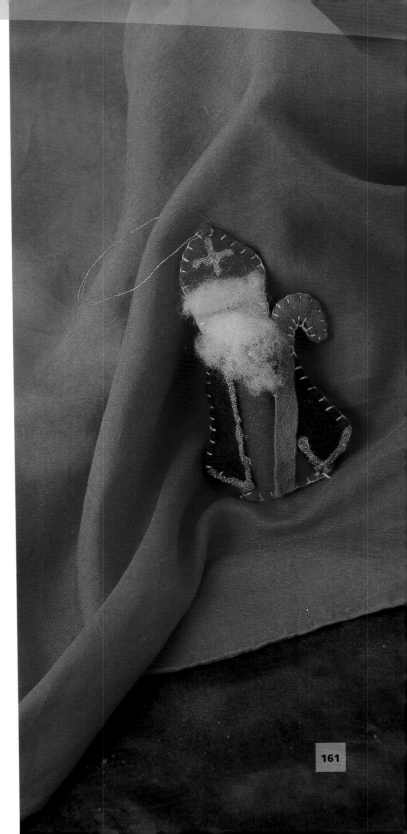

Shelly Franklin

Shelly added the beauty of flowers and design to school events.

In 1992, I was pushing 20-month-old Dominic in the stroller past Triangle Park and watched a cluster of parents and children with flowers in their hair celebrating Mayday. I thought it magical and then I saw that there were people I knew! Eleanor (Boogie) Jacobs from the Footloose crowd that I'd waited on at Pablo's for years; Betsy Engelman, who had taken a floral arts course from me; and CP Kanipe, who had been involved in co-housing for a while. I returned home and told David about it – but then we moved to Glenwood. When we moved back, we enrolled Dominic in CP's Waldorf kindergarten.

Each day we were surprised again by the great contrast between the Waldorf classes and the other programs in the Yellow Brick School. Every celebration, no matter how trivial, was also profound and you couldn't help but be affected. And the children were so happy to be

there! We had returned to Aspen to live "in community" and were actively engaged in the co-housing project, but we quickly found our real community at the school. We soon realized how important the work at the school was and we were amazed at the level of commitment from the founding families. We are glad we found it when Simone and Dominic were two and four rather than ten and twelve.

We didn't approach the school as an intellectually advanced institution because our children were little, nor did we have local Waldorf graduates as models. Still, it didn't feel like an experiment. The education had been around for seventy-five years and most important, it resonated in my heart. Though it hasn't always been smooth, my children avoided the harsh experiences so common in public schools. Both Simone and Dominic have had multiple teachers and Simone spent a year in another school where she got to try on another personality. She found she liked her Waldorf one better.

We have always been very involved parents and the festivals and fundraisers gave me an opportunity to join others in supporting the school. I've tried, especially, to carry beauty through the events. People notice the difference and our children grow up with a magical atmosphere surrounding them.

What I loved from the beginning I love still. Seeing my children with capes and crowns and a wooden sword at Michaelmas gave me goosebumps. It shaped them and is still in them. Watching performances in our amazing community hall is one of my favorite things. The image of Mr. Moore flitting across the stage remains very strong.

I have a box of the children's Waldorf treasures that speaks more loudly than any words about the value of the education – and how they have been valued by the education. It contains a baby bunting, a tooth pocket, a knitted chick, a gnome and gnome hammock, a felt bunny, a knitted mouse. Simone's "Little One" is a small rainbow doll made by her kindergarten teacher, Helena Hurrell, to accompany her to first grade. It still goes with me to watch Simone's plays. We may have spent their college money but I believed CP when she said that the solid, reverent foundation that they would receive would pave the way for their spiritual and academic life. Even now, they're sure of their world, their place in it, and themselves.

"I made myself a promise that I wouldn't forget..."

David Franklin

Shelly and David Franklin took an interest in the school before they were parents but their appreciation of Waldorf has deepened with their understanding.

I remember reading articles in the paper about a Waldorf school starting in 1990 and I thought, "That's exciting. Someone is doing something new in education," but I wasn't even a parent yet. Shelly and baby Dominic saw the Mayfaire celebration at Triangle Park but we moved to Glenwood. When we returned, we thought we'd join friends at the Early Learning Center for preschool but we found it to be a huge Fisher-Price playpen. We were convinced to try Waldorf when we went into the kindergarten and saw how enchanting and unique it was for the young child to "dwell in the kingdom of childhood." It confirmed the intuitions and suspicions I'd had when I was in kindergarten: "I really like playing. Why don't we do more of if?" Here was a school that really wanted the children to play, that made it the main point of the kindergarten. Play should be the work of the young child.

As I thought ahead to the idea of eight grades in the Waldorf School, it made me think back to my own schooling. I was a good student and took part in everything my school had to offer. I was a runt, so wrestling was my only sport, but I was involved in student council, band and plays. Still, by my high school years, it all came apart. I felt everything around me had failed me. Maybe I was looking for someone to blame but I felt institutionalized in high school, an "alienated youth." I could see then the importance of a system that takes a real interest in every child. Somewhere in high school I made myself a promise that I wouldn't forget that and somehow, when I got a chance, I would do something about it.

In the kindergarten it's all delightful, but when you begin having conversations about anthroposophy, the philosophy behind the education, you start to become a student yourself. I remember comparing biographical notes with Kathryn King one day. I said, "I think I was about 28 before I felt like I was really an independent functioning person. I could keep a job, pay my rent, cook for myself, do my laundry and take care of myself in the world." Kathryn told me that at the end of your fourth seven-year cycle your guardian angel takes a big step back and allows you more room to make more of your own decisions – and your own mistakes. It was another hook that said, "You mean this already makes sense to someone?" I started to turn over my own history and looked at some of those cornerstone years. I was married at 35 and had other important events at each seven-year cycle.

I got involved in teaching by doing woodworking projects at Mayfaire. Kate Friesen then asked if I would fill in for her when their family was on sabbatical from 1998 to '99. I thought, "What business do I have being a teacher?" – and sometimes

I still think that – but I agreed and enrolled in the applied sculptural arts course at Sunbridge College. The class had begun the year before so I got special treatment in the beginning. In the end, I was the veteran for the new class. Being a part-time teacher is having one foot on the boat, one on the dock. It's challenging and I have late nights before class trying to get everything together. A lot of my energy goes into schlepping. I'm keeping my fingers crossed that there is going to be a woodworking cabin soon.

I really think Waldorf is the most important work our family is doing. All this other busy work of keeping the mortgage paid and buying groceries is expected, but the real reason we're here is what is behind Waldorf education. After the early grades, we thought we'd try to continue our spiritual exploration at church but we concluded that it was another organization we couldn't keep up with and really, the kids' spiritual life and ours is filled at the school. Spirituality lives in the education. We bring it home. It's all unified.

The Doors, by artist Bob Johnson

I was very honored and excited when I was approached about designing and building the entry doors for the new Waldorf School Community Hall. Our family has been involved with Waldorf since 1975. My daughter, Jill Scher, is now the handwork teacher and my son, Matt Johnson, teaches seventh grade.

I've been interested in the mythological history of the human family and particularly my own ancestry which includes Nordic and Celtic myth. I became fascinated with the Nordic image of the sacred world ash tree, *Yggdrasil* (see page 89). The design process was a cooperative one and evolved over a period of months. My original image was one of an arbor which the children would pass through on their way into the building. This was modified over time and became less of an arbor image than I had originally intended. The introduction of frosted glass enhanced the Nordic imagery. I was quite satisfied with the finished doors and hope they will be a gift to all the children who enter.

The Woodworking Curriculum

By David Franklin

Children really enjoy woodworking classes. A mathematics lesson is head work. A music class works more with heart forces as students learn to give feeling to sound. In woodworking it is the will that is put to task. You get to make something happen with your hands, to let something flow back out of you, to respond, react, cause transformation in the world.

We start with eggs in the fourth grade, a tradition that's taken on a life of its own. Fourth graders are so enthusiastic and the egg is such a lovable form. They really are the parents of their eggs. Shaped only with rasps and files, the project requires patience and determination. The work is steady, rhythmic. All of the essential elements of woodworking are contained in the egg: a rough piece of wood is converted to the shape its maker intends, polished smooth, and given a finish that protects and enhances the wood. Later projects just get more complicated.

The spoon is a logical progression in fifth grade because it has purpose and is the perfect marriage of convex, which they worked with in the egg, and concave. The students learn to use saws and carving gouges. When I began working in wood, everything was rectilinear or cubic: bookshelves, boxes. It took me a long time as a carpenter before I ventured into curved space. I like that these students have the experience of "thinking outside the box."

I don't have a set curriculum. I'm still trying a lot of different projects and some are duds. The biggest challenge is to find a project that the whole class likes and can carry through to the end. Then it's just a matter of keeping the energy up. The great thing about woodworking is that you usually know what you want it to look like, but often it doesn't look like that in the end. You have to be flexible and bend your ideas with the mistakes you make along the way, or with the things that just can't happen according to plan, or were harder than you thought, or took more time – or broke. Wood is a forgiving material. You can always fix it or do something different or even start over.

We did two opposing projects in the seventh grade. First, we took a field trip to a hillside of dead juniper and each found a piece of crooked wood. We tried to really look into the wood and discover what was there and how we could bring it out. Some kids were successful, some weren't. Then we made cubic puzzles with six sides planned to fit together with tooth patterns. One project was looking for a vision in the mist and then executing it; the other was clear thinking and working with exactitude and precision. Some years we've attempted to reflect something from the curriculum, such as mechanical toys which involve an understanding of physics.

I've gotten to the point as a teacher that within any given class I take the little miracles where they happen. The students are all going to have a breakthrough moment at some time, but their bumpy spoons today are a reflection of who they are today. I could have helped them out or harangued them but it would have been less their

own experience. I think woodworking classes are therapeutic because just being in there, whittling wood off a stick, does something for you. I wish I had more time in my classes to observe because someone trained in observation could really tell something significant about each child by watching them work with tools.

Nancy Blanning

Nancy has been an early childhood consultant to the school for the past decade.

My first encounter with the Aspen Waldorf School was a call from Patty Fox in 1990. She said, "I'm really interested in Waldorf education and want to start a school in Aspen. I'm teaching a class at CMC to interest parents." I gasped, "But what do you know about Waldorf?" She answered that she'd attended a ten-day class in California and had been doing some reading. I was dubious to say the least, but my colleague, Bill Fordham, saw great promise in the initiative and I've always been a little sorry I didn't see it then, too.

The school was a reality when I first came to talk to parents about early childhood and I was impressed with what had been accomplished. There was a faculty, enrollment, and such enthusiasm, optimism and passion. The faculty and board solved their problems or blazed through them. The school is filled with genuine warmth, friendliness and a feeling of community that is not found in too many settings today.

In 1998, after seventeen years of teaching kindergarten at the Denver Waldorf School, I began to focus on remedial work, sensory integration and individual assessments. I have worked with five different Waldorf schools, including the WSRF, where I have done the annual assessment of second graders for the past six years.

Every time I visit the Roaring Fork Valley I am impressed with how healthy the children look. Every school has children with learning challenges now but here, there's both the opportunity and the in-

sistence that children "work." They move, stomp, get wet and dirty. It's fun for everyone but for the child who needs it, it's therapeutic.

From the beginning I have seen a commitment to beauty that goes beyond what most schools are able to provide. In every project, from sombreros to felt slippers, there's the will to create a deep cultural experience. Added to that is an element of genuine artistry and such consciousness is a gift to the children. Last time I was visiting, the children were singing in their assembly. In spite of the sophistication that surrounds the community, the innocence and purity of the children's voices was the sweetest I've ever heard. I can feel in my fingertips how richly the children are met. I love to come here!

This school is blessed with exceptionally beautiful buildings that embody the spirit of Waldorf education. Every faculty member who works here is blessed by such a setting and also challenged by it – to teach well in these spaces you have to really stretch in your inner life and personal growth. Small schools like this one often offer small salaries and struggling teachers, but this faculty is very solid, very talented. They offer an antidote to the entitled lifestyle of the Roaring Fork Valley. The school requires an investment of the will in the hard work it is doing.

When the kindergarten was in Aspen, it was embedded in typical daycares. Not only were Patty and CP willing to be observed as an alternative, they radiated a different choice for young children. Quietly, respectfully, a kindergarten through eighth grade school grew from the inspiration of two mad women who refused to consider it a bad idea. Wow!

"Last time I was visiting, the children were singing in their assembly. In spite of the sophistication that surrounds the community, the innocence and purity of the children's voices was the sweetest I've ever heard."

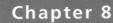

Chapter 8

The Teenager, Between Form and Freedom

The Aspen Waldorf School developed in stages very like a human being. In the first stage, between its birth in 1991 and its rebirth in 1997 as the Waldorf School on the Roaring Fork, the school developed its inner constitution and learned through communal "doing." It imitated established Waldorf schools, principally the traditions of the Denver Waldorf School, and passed on insights from the lectures and consultations of Eugene Schwartz, Merlyn and René Querido, Betty Staley and others. By the end of this phase, the school was established, though still familial.

In the next stage, between seven and fourteen, the school grew through imagination. Parents and faculty pictured what the school could be, and with substantial financial support from several families, began to color it in. As each building added a new dimension, the school was able to reach further into the community and with the completion of the Steven Moore Community Hall, the community could be welcomed in. As with the child, temperament dominated during these years and the school related to new families through feelings that were sometimes expressed in extremes.

Betty Staley wrote a very wise book for parents that summarizes the path to – and through – adolescence. In *Between Form and Freedom, A Practical Guide to the Teenage Years*, she says of the seven- to fourteen-year-old: "One hour they are happy; the next hour they are sad. They love you; they hate you. They say no; they say yes. They feel powerful; they feel powerless." The school experienced all of these extremes, especially between nine and twelve, but gradually strengthened its inner resources through the work of the community council, mentoring support team, faculty, board of trustees and parent council.

Now the school has crossed into adolescence. Greatly anticipated if not greatly feared by parents, the arrival of adolescence is a milestone in every child's life. Staley says that as parents, "[w]e have to be willing to make major changes in family life, to provide strong guidance, to ask hard questions, and to evaluate our priorities." As the school develops abstract thinking, it too will experience "the range of human emotions, ideals, goals and expressions of personality as it prepares for the spiritual birth of the individual self, the ego, somewhere around the twenty-first year." What guiding star will the school follow as it makes complex decisions for its future during the unpredictable teenage years? What is its goal for the future? What is the goal of any individuality?

"The whole object of the universe to us is the formation of character. If you think you came into being for the purpose of taking an important part in the administration of events, to guard a province of the moral creation from ruin, and that its salvation hangs on the success of your single arm, you have wholly mistaken your business."

Ralph Waldo Emerson

If this is so, decisions might be simplified by asking, "Will it build character?" One issue facing the school is the three-year process of becoming accredited through the Association of Waldorf Schools of North America and Association of Colorado Independent Schools, an arduous house-cleaning in which every aspect of the school is closely examined and evaluated. It can be disheartening – or it can be character building. Another decision likely to be made is expansion of the kindergarten program through satellites in other locations; another is building a high school. Will these decisions be made in a self-serving or selfless way? Will the school rise to the challenge of broadening its financial support in the local business community? Who will lead? Who will – once again – do the hard work?

173

Tim Connolly

Patti and Tim Connolly were founding parents of the Cedar Springs Waldorf School in California. They came to us for a year, as faculty chair and administrator, respectively, to lead the school into adolescence.

My year at the Waldorf School of the Roaring Fork was a golden one. It was an opportunity that I am pleased to have had. I arrived in the beginning of August and was offered three weeks to get acquainted with the tasks at hand in solitude, and to gain familiarity with my new surroundings. I was blessed to have the opportunity to work in a physical plant of such beauty and to work in a structure that was constructed with care, thoughtfulness and consciousness. I gazed out the window of my second story office too often and was led astray by the beauty of the surrounding mountains.

Patti and I grew to love the school community. As new members of the community, we were embraced by the parents and welcomed. The genuine friendliness of the community was overwhelming. Over time, we began to see how the spirit of the community reflected the values of the school and the school's founding families. Attending the parent council and community council meetings were something that I looked forward to. We appreciated the level of enthusiasm and the honesty that lived in these circles. We could not help but to think how much these values reflected those of the Sheffer's. Their undying support and love for the school was always so evident... their generosity inspiring.

It was difficult to leave the faculty in July. We worked hard together. Curricular standards were put into place. Common vision about teaching and educating lead to inspiring moments. The faculty meetings became fun and time not to be missed with colleagues. The eurythmy that was experienced was beyond what I had previously experienced at an elementary school. The music and movement classes offered the students opportunities to work with gifted teachers. The class plays were well done and the effect of this program over a student's eight-year experience at the school was felt by a moving production of Thornton Wilder's *Our Town* by the eighth grade. It was clear that the faculty overall wanted to improve and bring a balance of arts and academics to the students. We made difficult decisions together and learned how to trust each other's thoughts and opinions. Laughter filled our meetings and our last moments together.

Yet what would a school be without students? The students of the Roaring Fork school worked hard.

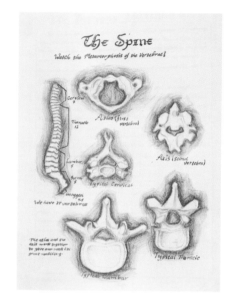

They strove to learn how to balance their work with play. Their shrieks of fun and laughter brought the necessary joy that needs be present in a school. Their beauty never echoed so loudly as when they sang the school song in unison in the acoustically perfect Steven Moore Hall. Their healthy faces wearing the rosy glow of a Colorado winter is paramount in my mind.

I believe an accreditation process would be valuable to the school. It would provide the community with a goal that would elevate the school to the level of truly being established. There are standards to be raised to achieve this goal, but worthy goals are not new to this community.

Robyn Myler

Robyn leads a new generation of parents. Neither a founder nor a builder, she will oversee the work of the board of trustees as adolescence begins.

My first child, a daughter, was born with a minor congenital defect. As a result of this trauma, I was sensitive to her needs and started searching for schools that would likewise be sensitive to her needs. I had two friends who had their children in the Waldorf preschool. As I listened to their arguments in favor of and against the educational philosophy at Waldorf, I solidified my own values regarding education and found that I agreed with the values of the friend who chose to continue with Waldorf education. Specifically, I disagreed with the friend who chose to transfer her child to a highly academic kindergarten where the child was skipped into first grade when he was not ready socially. So, in 1999, I enrolled my daughter with Christy Braeger in the Childrens' Garden, a toddler Waldorf program, where she stayed for two years. Then we came to the grade school and I've really never looked back.

I loved Ms. Braeger. My daughter was engaged and happy and made nice friends – and I met nice adults. I learned more about my daughter's temperament from Ms. Braeger in those two years than from all the books I had read about child development. Her words struck me as true and heartfelt and loving. The values spoke to me and helped me to solidify my value system. I had become fairly well-educated in the current theories of child development but this, I thought, was the real thing. Waldorf's philosophy felt deeper and richer and truer.

My daughter is now in third grade and my son is in first grade at Waldorf. They are both highly engaged in their classes. I attended an academically demanding private school and I feel that my experience was limiting. I'm glad for my children to have a variety of friends from all walks of life whom I believe will be their life-long friends. I never had that opportunity because my schools were so competitive that as soon as we graduated, we all went our separate ways. Further, I can see that my children will gain a comprehensive education that not only challenges them academically, but also encourages them to establish a firm value system, just as I was encouraged to do as a parent choosing a school.

When we came to the main school, I saw the need for help and I was willing to help. With my strong voice for the parents, I was invited to join parent council. When Jennifer Schiller stepped down as chairperson, she saw I had a vision of what parent council could become and she asked me to replace her. I worked to bring more form and more energy to the group in my two years in that position.

As a lawyer, I have a traditional business sense and so learning to work in the Waldorf way, using consensus, was challenging at times. I was concerned about the lack of leadership at the school but when I looked at its history, I could see that there had been strong leadership in the past. I felt that it would bubble to the surface again. This year, there is much more enthusiasm for leadership. With the help of such leadership, the school is becoming renowned in the local community and the greater Waldorf community, getting what it deserves because of the support of hundreds of dedicated people.

I served on the board of trustees for two years, became vice president and am now board president. I think I have the energy and the vision but I'll need support to do this job well. These past two years, the board and school councils have worked to create a five-year strategic plan that was finalized at our last Janus meeting. I'd like to see that plan completed. It focuses on increasing enrollment through enhancing faculty training and experience, school accreditation and outreach to the greater Roaring Fork community.

The viability of starting a Waldorf high school seems to be a question on many parents' minds. It is my feeling that the elementary school needs to be at full enrollment of two hundred students before this occurs, because the elementary school income will be needed to support the financial needs of a high school. This looks promising but no one can predict the future. In order to support enrollment, the long-range plan seeks to establish a Waldorf kindergarten in Glenwood Springs as early as next year. But I do believe that our next five-year plan will include the building of a Waldorf high school.

"I have a vision of what it can become."

177

Karen Draper

"We wanted a gentle education."

Karen and Willie Draper have quietly, kindly and consistently supported the school since 1998.

We came to the valley in 1998 with the sole purpose of putting Wolfie in the Waldorf school because we wanted a gentle education for him. We had met Philip Incao, our anthroposophic doctor, through an osteopath in Boulder. The summer we arrived, we worked with Keith Schlussler in the garden, pressed apple cider with Helena Hurrell, and loved the natural feeling of the straw-bale building. We didn't have a lot to go on, but met Christy Braeger and enrolled Wolfie in her Flying Fish kindergarten. Despite the fact that Wolfie had ankle surgery and was in a leg cast, we felt he was safe and nurtured with Christy and we were nurtured by the packets of information that Christy gave us to read about child development and Waldorf education.

The next year we enrolled Wolfie with CP at the school kindergarten. That summer, Willie was the "volunteer coordinator" for the new kindergarten building and so we became very involved. I've been on the board of trustees for three years now and am still learning how I can help. My first real contribution was the silent auction in the new Community Hall. We made $25,000 and were so proud of ourselves. This year, only three years later, we grossed over $50,000!

Wolfie's class has had two teachers, Patty Doyle and Julianna Lichatz. I believe in the school, the curriculum and the teachers. I'm in awe of what they try to accomplish with young people in drama, music, handwork and all of the academic subjects. It's great the way it has grown in numbers and prominence. It will soon be full and we'll be talking about a high school.

Carla Beebe Comey

Carla's breadth of experience brings depth to the life of the school.

"I always felt I came 'home' to anthroposophy."

I started tutoring when I was in middle school and knew then I wanted to be a teacher. But when I left home at 16 and began working my way through an education program in college, I was disappointed in what I found. Still, I did just about everything I could do without a teaching credential. I worked in a resident home with handicapped boys, ran an after-school program, guided school groups through the Exploratorium in San Francisco. By the summer of 1981, I decided I would complete my education doing an inter-collegiate independent program in Boston and my thesis would be "The History of Human Consciousness through the Arts." While looking for the college where I would study, I attended a music and dance workshop in Cape Cod and met Roberto Trostli, who was becoming a master Waldorf teacher and is now a Waldorf writer as well. When I told him my quest he said, "You might be interested in the kind of schools I teach in." We spent four hours sitting on a dock while he gave me a lecture on Rudolf Steiner, his view of child development and Waldorf education. I had found what I was truly looking for.

I moved to Boston, read the books Roberto had recommended and called Anna Rainville at the Lexington Waldorf School. I told her I wanted to teach in the school and she invited me to an open house. When I stepped into the kindergarten, I nearly burst into tears; it was so beautiful. Within weeks, I was teaching there part-time, had joined an anthroposophical study group and had begun to read Rudolf Steiner, setting myself a goal of fifty pages a day. Roberto kept track of me, and the following spring asked if I would consider caring for Arvia Ege, one of the first American Waldorf teachers and a poet. I moved in with Arvia and her sister and brother-in-law, Christy and Henry Barnes, whom I still think of as my anthroposophical grandparents. Henry was chairman of the Anthroposophical Society in America and I was exposed to many influential anthroposophists who came from around the world to visit.

180

In 1983, I went to Emerson College in England to begin my foundation year and lived in the home of John Davy, formerly a science editor for the London Observer who had come to direct the foundation year. (His wife wrote *Lifeways*, a well-loved parenting book.) Because of my interest in folk dancing and music, I was drawn to eurythmy and applied with 200 others to the eurythmy school in The Hague – because most of the people there had short hair and their feet on the ground! Although Werner Barford accepted me as one of his twenty-two new students, it was not to be. Before the course started, I traveled to India with a group from Emerson to help conduct a conference for Indian teachers interested in Waldorf education and there I contracted hepatitis. I spent a year recovering, half at home and half at Rudolf Steiner College in Sacramento studying the arts – when I was awake! I stayed for the teacher training, which included kindergarten, before I felt well enough to study eurythmy. I transferred to Spring Valley and studied privately with Kari van Ort, a eurythmist of real force. In 1990, I returned to Emerson to study pedagogical eurythmy with Molly von Heider.

Mid-school year, 1990-91, the Cape Ann Waldorf School needed a eurythmy teacher and I had connections to friends there from Emerson College and my India experience, so I taught eurythmy from January to June. The next year, they needed a fourth grade teacher so I taught fourth grade and continued with the class through eighth, all the while teaching eurythmy. After my class graduated, I thought I would at last be just a eurythmy teacher, but I agreed to cover a fourth grade for half a year. I then broke my foot and spent another half year teaching eighth grade and thinking if I ever wanted to be a eurythmy teacher I would have to leave that school!

I moved to Oregon and taught just eurythmy in two schools, a sabbatical! But I tired of the rain and I was ready to deepen my relationship with Rob Comey, whom I'd met years before and who had settled in the Roaring Fork Valley. Steven Moore and I talked and talked on the phone and after a visit, I came to the school full-time in October, 2001.

The school was again in transition. Bill Fordham, Rochelle Chayet and I formed the mentoring support team to help guide the teachers and I assisted with bringing in outsiders to mentor. The next year, the faculty was shaken by the loss of several more teachers, but I felt the model we were forming with the mentoring support team and the community council was really healthy if we could just get healthy within it. To me the two organs felt like the two arms of a college of teachers, the traditional leadership in Waldorf schools. To have the mentoring support team focusing solely on the pedagogy and the community council taking more of an administrative role was exciting. The community council was a great group of dedicated parents and teachers who threw themselves into the school.

Further, they took the time to understand a bit about anthroposophy and what needed to be done to help the school grow into a true Waldorf school. They did this without feeling they needed to control the pedagogy and I really think the present structure is the healthiest I've seen in a Waldorf school.

I always felt I came "home" to anthroposophy. I soaked it up and to this day, twenty-four years later, I've never felt I needed to step back from it. Nor have I needed to step back from the world in which we live. Anthroposophy has, in fact, allowed me to live more fully in this world and helped me to understand and appreciate it in all of its complexity. I am grateful to have found anthroposophy so long ago.

Jane Pargiter-Hatem

Jane Pargiter-Hatem – what tenacity! She supported the school when it began, before she had children. She supports it still and will continue to do so.

"I observed at Powder Pandas when the school first opened."

My connection with Waldorf dates back to 1978 when my parents considered sending me to a Waldorf high school in Mbabane, Swaziland. So, when my friend CP Kanipe told me she and two other Pattys were starting a Waldorf school in Aspen, my interest was piqued and I sat in and observed the first days of the school at Powder Pandas with the thought that one day I too might become a Waldorf teacher. My background is in tertiary education and I missed teaching. Eugene Schwartz came to the valley as a guest speaker and his advice was, "You're newly married. Wait. Have your family, then decide." I am so grateful to him! The responsibilities of being both a Waldorf teacher and a Waldorf parent can be overwhelming, and I have great admiration for those who love this school enough to do both.

Knowing that Steiner's philosophies melded with my beliefs of how to educate children, I put my daughter Tamsin on the "waitlist" when she was born. CP howled with laughter when I called. "Don't we wish!" she said. Fourteen years later, the waiting list is imperative for the earlier grades!

Tamsin started preschool the same year the school moved to its mid-valley location. The Aspen Waldorf preschool provided Tamsin with a wonderful grounding; her first school years were spent with Julie McCallan, then Helena Hurrell and finally with dear Cathy Fisher. Tessa, my second daughter followed suit, ending her pre-school years with CP and Patty Fox in their independent Aspen Children's Garden. It was difficult for me when the AWS found property to build on 22 miles away (downvalley) from our upvalley home; however, the benefits of the beautiful campus far outweigh the negatives. The children have grass to play on, instead of being snowbound in Aspen for the long winter months, and they have wonderful wetlands and wooded areas to explore. I compared the time my neighbors' children spend on their circuitous bus route to the Aspen schools and realized my girls' trip downvalley to Carbondale is only ten minutes longer.

Tamsin started first grade with Bill Fordham and they had and still have a deep connection. When we visited Bill in New York last summer, they spent the whole day immersed in each other, walking and talking their way around the Spring Valley campus. Bill taught me to love and understand anthroposophy and Waldorf education. Matt Johnson, Tamsin's teacher for the last four years is like a young Bill Fordham and he tells me Tamsin is there to remind him he doesn't know it all yet! She has a sweet heart but an acerbic tongue and yet she receives constant compliments from our friends because her personality is allowed to shine through every day. Tessa, in first grade, loves the diverse outdoor experience she gets at school every day and is lovingly held and guided by her teacher, Heather Handy.

I think Waldorf reminds me of the well-rounded education I received in South Africa, with strong academics but emphasis on outdoor activities too: gardening, hiking, skiing, field trips, a strong balance between the physical and mental faculties. Thinking about the changes the last hundred years has brought to our world and knowing that change continues to accelerate, I believe that being well-rounded, flexible and versatile are some of the most important characteristics we can cultivate and Waldorf Education speaks strongly to developing well-rounded, well-adjusted children and young adults.

I would certainly like to see the school buy neighboring property but I think building a high school can wait a while longer. The existing school must be solidified in all its facets. We need to support a stronger faculty, birth a college of teachers, perhaps offer biodynamic farming with animals of our own, and think about teacher housing. Then, perhaps, we can think about developing a high school.

Mary Wentzel

"I'm here because the education has soul."

Mary arrived at Waldorf with the millennium.

I'm the naysayer. I always have to question things, which is why I co-created a book study group for parents. The group evolved from an education conference I attended in Boulder. By good fortune, I met Barbara Rose Balock and the two of us put our hearts and heads together, opening the doors to anyone interested in child-rearing information. The book club has read and discussed many great books including *Endangered Minds* by Jane Healy, *Navigating the Terrain of Childhood* by Jack Petrash, *Between Form and Freedom* by Betty Staley and *The Recovery of Man in Childhood* by A.C. Harwood. With each book I feel more convinced that the Waldorf approach is the right one for us. I'm here because the education has soul.

I first learned of Waldorf from a friend who home-schooled her children using a Waldorf curriculum. Those children are bright, articulate adults now and played significant roles in their class plays as well as being class valedictorians. When our daughter Jillian was a baby, we met Julie Mulcahy, who encouraged me to enroll in an introductory class for parents taught by Patty Fox. I later enrolled Jillian in Christy Braeger's Waldorf kindergarten class. Now she's in Heather Handy's class. Although Waldorf is right for Jillian, I'm mindful of whom I tell about Waldorf education. A lifetime of open-hearted seeking brought me to Waldorf but others arrive at different destinations.

Mary Wentzel, Renee Ramge and Sarah Liotta

Sarah Liotta

Sarah and Tito Liotta are ready for the work that lies ahead.

"I think that Waldorf has the strongest curriculum in the valley."

I first heard of the Waldorf School through an acquaintance who spoke of her daughter learning German – and violin! I think that Waldorf has the strongest curriculum in the valley. It is the only school that offers foreign languages, music, art, movement, drama, handwork and woodwork to every child. When we saw the campus, thirteen acres with wetlands and beautiful buildings, we were convinced. My husband, Tito, an orthopedic surgeon, surprised me with his enthusiasm because, obviously, the arts aren't his background. The more we learned, the more we liked, but we never imagined what an effect it would have on us as parents.

Mikaela started in the kindergarten with Ms. Christy and the boys, triplets, started with Rochelle Chayet. I especially liked that the teachers wanted us to keep the boys together. We listened and took the advice they offered, turned off the TV, fed the children at 5:30 and put them to bed at 7:00. They thrived. I learned more about my children at parent conferences than I would have suspected. It's humbling that someone else knows your children so well.

Our second year, Robyn Myler asked me to join parent council and now Jane Pargiter-Hatem and I co-chair it. Jane and I are a good team and – after our trip to South Africa together – we co-chaired Mayfaire, too! Tito has now joined the board of trustees but we can't think of a better way to invest our time. Our children are so important to us.

For the future, we'd love to see a high school. We need full enrollment first but I think that's coming faster than we've planned. The word is out; we're on the map. Experienced, accredited teachers want to come here. We need a larger, more involved board and a broader parent council with two active members from each class. We need to network with other Waldorf schools rather than reinvent the wheel. We need to broaden our base of financial support. Educational institutions need financial support from a wide variety of sources: grants, individual donors, grandparents, businesses and fundraisers. There's work to do and Tito and I are ready to do it.

"Could I have found the fortitude to stick
with something so idealistic and difficult?
If I could have had such faith, I would owe it
to Patty Fox and CP Kanipe."

Stewart Oksenhorn

Stewart's daughter, Olivia, attended the Aspen Chirdren's Garden, an independent preschool taught by Patty Fox and CP Kanipe from 2001 to 2004. When she transferred to the Waldorf School on the Roaring Fork, Stewart began the journey forward through the grades as well as the journey back through the history as editor of *Raising Waldorf*.

Reading and editing the stories of the founders – builders and board members, teachers and parents – of the Waldorf School on the Roaring Fork, I am struck by two things: how different their stories are from my own. And how familiar they are.

When my wife Candice and I placed our daughter Olivia in the Waldorf School on the Roaring Fork kindergarten, there were no questions of the school's stability or its structure, its history or its future. What we saw was a stunning building, capable and caring teachers like Brian Sweeterman (could a kindergarten teacher have a better name than Sweeterman?) and Verita Malin her class teacher, and an atmosphere of serenity that comforted our daughter and ourselves. The thought of where the school had come from, what sort of effort it might have taken, never crossed my mind. It was a school, and schools just happen, right?

Reading about Patty Fox's Waldorf classes at Colorado Mountain College and the first Mayfaires, dwindling enrollments and the failed initiative with the public schools, teachers going off to be educated and parents raising the Waldorf School on the Roaring Fork buildings, I learned how wrong I was. I am dumbfounded by the effort, audacity, generosity and sheer will of those who made this school. It makes me think I got off easy, and that I missed something infinitely valuable as well. Could I have found the fortitude to stick with something so idealistic and difficult?

If I could have had such faith, I would owe it to Patty Fox and CP Kanipe. The way our family came to these two wise, wonderful women is what resonates with all the other stories in this book. Waldorf seemed to have found us, just as it did so many others.

When Olivia was three and a half, we weren't thinking yet of pre-school. We had a great baby-sitter, Julia, to help Candice out with our very tenacious child. But when Julia got word that her father was ill, and would have to return to New Zealand months before planned, we had to rethink things quickly. Candice suggested the Children's Garden, about which I knew only that it was conveniently located in the Yellow Brick Building, a few minutes from our house and two blocks from my office. I knew nothing about Waldorf at the time.

I couldn't have had a better intro-duction than Patty and CP. Their classroom was a reflection of them: warm, gentle and calm. I could not have felt better about leaving Olivia in their hands. I slowly learned bits and pieces of Steiner's philosophy, but seeing Olivia happy, having her teach us songs and meal-time blessings, was all I needed. Thanks to Patty and CP, I went from suspi-cious to grateful. For me, the two years she spent in Children's Gar-den could have gone on forever.

But of course, they couldn't. And Waldorf didn't seem an option for kindergarten and grade-school, given the commute from Aspen and the cost. We settled on the Aspen Community School.

Until two days before classes start-ed. Candice came to me one night and said she had serious second thoughts about Olivia's schooling. The next day, we unenrolled Olivia from the Community School; the day after that, we sent her 25 miles downvalley to WSRF.

What a privilege it has been to have Olivia in an environment that stresses play, health, the outdoors and the imagination. Both Candice and I lamented that our schooling didn't inspire us to love learning. But Olivia adores going to school, loves her first-grade lessons in movement, Spanish and eurythmy. I am indebted to the bold people who paved this path, and made it so much easier for us to follow.

Doug Sheffer

It is in giving that we truly set the forces of creativity and freedom in motion.

In the end, what brought me to the Waldorf school was my love of theater. It was a long road, which started as an unfulfilled desire to act during my high school years in Connecticut. In 1965, I would hide backstage doing production work and secretly wish I was on stage. Through college in Pennsylvania I studied pre-architecture and graphic design but never forgot that desire.

Twenty five years later, my wife Barbi and I attended Merlyn and René Querido's first workshop on Star Mesa (near Aspen) in July of 1990 and then enrolled in Patty Fox's class at CMC. As new parents, we were ready for the change of lifestyle parenting brings and found that Waldorf encompassed everything we were looking for: a community of peers with children and a spiritual approach to life. It was instantly clear that Waldorf was perfect for us and we never turned back.

Concurrent to our daughter Brooke's enrollment in the Aspen Waldorf School, two things happened to me: I auditioned for several plays at a local community theater and I met Steven Moore and Valerie Lee. The combination of these two events would set me on a adult course of study, which would change my life. Being involved with the founding of the school has been a coming-out of sorts, a maturing. I was able to feel part of a group, especially in my association with Steven and Valerie helping to plan and produce plays for grades 1-8 at the school. These were the heydays, which culminated in the construction of the community hall building and the naming of the performance space after Steven in honor of his life's work in speech, drama, Eurythmy, directing and playwriting.

It has been pointed out that our community did not found our Waldorf school out of a strong anthroposophical impulse and it is true that we didn't start with years of study. But there are two ways to approach Steiner's work. One is study and the other is rolling up one's sleeves and getting to the task at hand. We had a lot of heart, a lot of will, and a desire to create a school out of our love for the children. There were many supporters with strong anthroposophical background guiding us from a distance. I think it is significant that most of the first families have remained friends throughout the fourteen years. Working together in the parent body with focused intention, and being able to look each other in the eye every day, is as important as having the school.

On the practical level, we ended up with a building committee embedded in the school when we moved it from Aspen to Carbondale in 1997. Stephen Kanipe, a founder, was head of the building department in

Aspen and knew all about alternative materials and shepherding approvals through the bureaucracy. The fist contractor, Matt Flink, came to us through Bill Engelman, another founder and local contractor. Laura Bartels-Struempler and Chuck Cole, both parents, took over from there. Jeff Dickinson, our architect, found us for his daughter just as we found him for his green architecture. We had a parent plumber in Patrick Johnson. Finally, Bob Schultz brought a "big-picture" approach to the design process with his regional planning background. There were others, of course, who filled in with much needed skills.

The founders devoted the first six years to lovingly creating rhythmic support for their "child," the new school. At seven years (when all the child's old cells had been replaced) we moved and started building a new physical body to house the school. It grew more beautiful with each addition, surrounding us with healthy forms and vibrant colors. It also received the energy we expended to do the inner work of emotional or astral development. That work is still continuing, focused and fortified, as we go through the process of accreditation by the Association of Waldorf Schools of North America and the Colorado Association of Independent Schools. When we finish this process, we will be more self-aware, ready to go forward with our ego work. Then I would like to see the school reach out to the greater Roaring Fork Valley community in the areas of arts and service.

We are already seeing some shifts in the school financially. A Waldorf school sits squarely in the cultural realm and relies for a portion of its revenues on the excess funds generated in the financial or business realm. Many who can afford to do so contribute to our giving campaigns. In recent years, alumni and grandparents have become a larger source of support for the school. I would like to see that expanded into increased partnership with area businesses.

Personally, I feel honored to have been able to fund aspects of the school out of a family foundation. My grandfather was an immigrant who worked in the early 1900's to house other immigrants in New York City. His holdings were the basis of the Betty R. Sheffer Family Foundation, named after my mother. She instilled in me from an early age that philanthropy was an important part of life. It is in giving that we truly set the forces of creativity and freedom in motion. My mom died prematurely of cancer at 54 years and our community hall is a way of memorializing her love of children, education and the arts. Although she never met my daughter, wife or Steven Moore, she would have liked them. They are shining examples of what she held so dear in life; warm, loving, giving individuals who would do anything to help support accomplishing unfulfilled goals. I see this in many of the members of our Waldorf community too. Maybe that's why I am still involved even though our daughter graduated long ago. There's a lot of work still to be done.

"When Waldorf grabs you, it grabs you hard."

Chapter 9

The Graduates

"You will know them by their fruits."
Matthew 7:16

As the school begins its third seven-year cycle (fourteen to twenty-one), many of the first graduates are completing theirs. We do not yet know what fruits they will bear or what seeds they will plant, but their blossoms are widely colored, exciting, hopeful.

Though not without trauma, the WSRF graduates' teenage years have been without tragedy. They've scattered into seven private and public high schools where they quickly became class officers, team captains, academic stars, instrumental and vocal soloists, and leads in class plays. They involved themselves in community service and graduating seniors have won countless awards and scholarships. All of the high school graduates are attending or will attend colleges of their choice.

This is a sampling from the "founding" graduates as their stories unfold.

Marina Kanipe O'Keefe

Her father, Stephen, likes to say that Marina was "the first tooth," the only graduate of the Aspen Waldorf School.

Of course I was worried when I started high school, coming from sixth grade at the Waldorf school. The first few weeks, I was a wreck. I had a very hard English teacher who completely intimidated me and I decided to transfer into an easier class. It was really too basic – crossword puzzles – but it gave me a chance to figure out high school and after that, I was on honor roll all four years. I joined the Outreach Club, Heroes and MAC (Making a

Commitment to avoid alcohol and drugs). I played softball, became manager of the baseball team and was active in Young Life. I was also working at the Columbine Shop, then the Rocky Mountain Chocolate Factory and Short Sport, and baby-sitting. I was busy!

I attended Roanoke College in Virginia but after 9/11, it was too far from home for me and for my parents. I transferred to the University of Northern Colorado in

Marina Kanipe's graduation, 1997

Greeley, then to Mesa State College in Grand Junction. I knew all along that I wanted to teach preschool and I was frustrated by the poor counseling I received that kept me from reaching my goal. I wanted to come home for another reason, too. I had met my future husband, Tim O'Keefe, and we were married the summer of 2005.

I'm teaching my first class of 3-year olds this year without a B.A., but with the intention of completing one and earning a preschool director's license in the next few years. I'm borrowing from Waldorf in my classroom, removing extra toys and posters, draping playstands and singing a lot. I think I most appreciate the simplicity of the Waldorf school. I want it to play not only a large part in my classroom but also in my personal life. I appreciate other things we hated in the process, like eurythmy, and now find the well-roundedness of my Waldorf education, combining bookwork with handwork, invaluable. In the future, I'll focus on my family and hope to open a childcare program of my own.

Hannah Grenfell

Hannah was the first graduate of the Waldorf School on the Roaring Fork, in May of 1998.

I left the Waldorf School with many unforgettable memories, but one of my fondest is our trip to Ashland, Oregon, for the Shakespeare Festival. We rode the train from Glenwood Springs to Reno and I remember loving the sound of the train wheels on the tracks and sitting in the observation car with the rest of the class to look out over the landscape. It felt like looking at a painting. We rented a van in Reno and from there to Ashland, the ride seemed very long. Mrs. Fox made it easier by reading to us – someone else drove – and I even remember the name of the book, *Naya Nuki*. The hills of Ashland looked to me like every picture of Ireland I had ever seen. The leaves on the trees in the park were bigger than my head and the air smelled damp and cold. The play I remember most was *A Midsummer Night's Dream*. I still remember what the costumes and lighting looked like. I thought the play was outstanding and it left me in awe, definitely inspired to pursue a life in theater. There are many things I remember from that trip, but mostly I think of how much it

impacted my life. I learned that there are amazing experiences to be had outside of your own little realm of existence and if you explore them, they might just change your life.

I'm now a senior studying theatre at Mesa State College and on the president's list with a GPA of 3.93. I'm taking lessons in dance and vocal performance as well as theater. This summer I interned with a real estate broker in Aspen and have broadened my options to include real estate as well as professional acting.

Maureen Fox

Maureen was the oldest of the "first four" – Maureen, Melinda, Emily and Alex – who started first grade in the first class and graduated from eighth grade.

Maureen Fox in a eurythmy performance at the Aspen Youth Center

Time, in my life, is continually fleeting and never seems to pause long enough for me to grasp it or to offer me a chance to look back on what has passed. Now I have the opportunity to pause only for a moment and look back on what has so quickly become my Waldorf past. It has been seven terribly short, but tremendously full years since I graduated with my teacher/mother's first class of graduates from the Waldorf School on the Roaring Fork. I went to Aspen High School with concern about my performance in a public school and found that I had been fully prepared by my time at the Waldorf school to manage my class load. I found too that I had gained other character traits which became strikingly evident in the new landscape of high school. One that stands out to me now is an active imagination which led not only to my achieving good grades, but also acknowledgement in student senate, on various planning committees, backstage with performances, and in the Aspen Youth Council. I was able to help create activities and organize events in a manner

that interested other students and was appreciated by faculty and administration. My activities resulted in my being awarded a Leadership and Service Scholarship when I entered Lewis & Clark College in Portland, Oregon.

Along with an inspired imagination, I have discovered since graduating from the Waldorf school that I have a passion for travel and exploration. I find myself most contented when I am in the most unfamiliar territory, which in the past seven years has ranged from navigating the largest cities in Europe, to selling strawberries in Scotland's rural farmland, and mountaineering and sea kayaking through Alaska's vast wilderness.

While I am majoring in English, my plan for the future has yet to be revealed. I will spend five months in a language intensive and volunteer program in Buenos Aires, Argentina, before returning to L&C to finish my undergraduate degree, and I have no doubt the direction of my life will be revealed to me as time continues to hasten past.

Melinda Engelman

Melinda was the heart of the first class.

Songs in the mornings, blessings before meals, creating my own text books – this was what I knew as a child in a Waldorf school. To some children, the rituals and teaching methods would be viewed as unusual or strange, but looking back, those "strange" methods shaped me into the person that I am today: creative, passionate and a leader of those around me.

I was in the first graduating class at the Waldorf School on the Roaring Fork. After attending kindergarten in the Aspen public school my mother said, "I do not want my child sitting in front of the TV in her classroom!" She and a few other parents decided to start a Waldorf school in Aspen. My class was very small at first and I became very close to my classmates, two of whom are still my best friends. Being the "guinea pigs" of the school, as we were always called, we had to depend on each other for support and encouragement.

Some of my fondest memories are of the seasonal festivals. In the fall, I looked forward to Michaelmas. I vividly remember making dragon kites and trying to fly them in the cool, crisp air, stumbling over the red and yellow leaves covering the ground. During the dark, cold winter, I looked forward to the Advent Garden. It was a mystical experience, walking into a candle-lit room with a pine bough spiral covering the floor. I would patiently wait for the beautiful angel all in white to

Melinda Engelman at Mayfaire in Aspen

"Cactus Flowers," 7th grade Utah backpacking trip

come into the room singing. She would calmly take each of us from our chairs and lead us through the spiral to the candle in the center. I was the curious child who would walk very slowly, looking at all the little treasures that were placed among the pines. But spring has always been my favorite time of year and when the bulbs popped up and the sun started to feel warmer, I knew May Day was around the corner. I wore my prettiest spring dress and danced the maypole carrying a brightly colored ribbon as if I were the princess of the school. I stood tall to be sure that the flower crown that I'd worked on so diligently would not fall off my head.

At 20, I think back to my childhood and how lucky I was to have had a Waldorf education. Yes, it was very different and as a child I was not always sure that "different" was a good thing. Now, however, I can

proudly say that it was. In high school, I created artistic presentations and was an event organizer able to stand in front of the class and speak about ideas and plans. I was my class vice president, president of the Aspen Youth Council and a member of the Aspen Jewish Congregation Board of Directors. I received the 2003 Leadership Award at Aspen High School. This involvement and these strengths have continued with me into college. I am now attending the University of San Francisco, where I am a communications major with a double minor in public relations and media studies.

I believe that my Waldorf education gave me self-confidence, the ability to express myself clearly and respect for those around me. These were taught by positive role models who really cared about me and my education.

Mariah Mulcahy

Mariah joined the first class after three years in the Cedar Springs Waldorf School.

The Waldorf school has been a part of my life since I can remember and it has shaped me into the person I am today. At a young age, the Waldorf school helped me to identify my strengths and grow with them. It allows children to develop naturally and embrace what nature has given them. In my particular situation, I found a true passion and love for sports and art. Artistically, I owe it all to my beloved teacher, Steven Moore. He taught me about the mind and body working together as well as my outer space, the bubble around me that I can control.

I have taken it all with me as I've grown from a teenager into a young adult. My passions have changed from being a basketball and soccer star in high school to now loving fashion and design. I plan to complete a Masters degree in Interior Design at the University of Colorado in Boulder and am grateful to my Waldorf education and my dear mother for my drive and passion.

Trojan Horse at Wintersköll snow sled contest

Mariah Mulcahy, left, and Emily DeLise, right, at the University of Colorado at Boulder.

Emily DeLise

Emily's unique Waldorf education led to her title of "Most Individual" in the Aspen High School year book.

It's different for me now that I've left the Waldorf school, but one of the things I loved best was that I knew everyone: every teacher, every student at the school. And I loved having the same people in my class year after year.

When our class graduated in 1999, every single one of us was in advanced classes in high school. Now we're all doing amazing things in college. Anyone who is doubtful of this alternative education should look at that. It wasn't that we were all so bright, but we all got a really good foundation and loved learning.

Emily DeLise's painting was chosen as the Aspen High Season's Greetings Card for 2002

Art was my favorite subject. I loved drawing the pictures for our own textbooks, illustrating all of the lessons, painting and sculpting. I'm deciding now between a fine arts or art history major but want to incorporate the business of art into my studies, too. I've transferred from Fort Lewis to the University of Colorado this fall and am looking forward to the wider range of classes I'll have available.

*Left: Patty Fox's fifth grade class performs **Perseus and Andromeda** at Paepcke Auditorium in Aspen*

Below: Emily as Medusa and Keegan Doble as Perseus.

197

The founders in 8th grade. Top row: Mariah Mulcahy, Emily DeLise, Alexandria Fortier. Bottom row: Melinda Engelman, Maureen Fox

Alexandra Fortier

Alexandra was another one of the "founders," starting in first grade and traveling straight through eighth. She's continued to achieve the goals she sets for herself.

When I first left the Waldorf school I was scared going to Aspen High School. I worried about tests and grading but it wasn't that bad. Since I graduated, I've come to really appreciate the Waldorf school. This year in college I was randomly assigned a roommate – another Alexandra – who went to Shining Mountain Waldorf School in Boulder for twelve years. It's been very cool to live with another Waldorf student and we've had a chance to talk a lot about it. We both feel we were prepared in ways that we weren't even aware of at the time – like not to freak out when things go wrong and instead look for solutions. I also think that Alexandra and I both care about people in ways that others don't. We're more open to other people and ideas, and I think we're kinder.

The artistic part of the curriculum helped me tremendously in architecture at the University of Colorado, although it's been challenging at times. Last year I broke my wrist skiing and so much of our work is drawing, it really set me back. Too, what we work on is often very abstract. I wonder how it's ever going to relate. So I've questioned my course at times but I've never changed directions.

The best part of my education has been interning for the past four summers with an architect in Aspen. She went to CU, too, and experienced some of the same frustrations. I plan to continue to work with her and then possibly start my own firm specializing in residential architecture. There are many ways to go in architecture. With my Aspen mentor, my CU counselor and my dad advising me, I feel good about the future.

Brittany Fortier

Waldorf education has given Brittany an interest in the world, from the basketball court to Ireland.

When I left the protected environment of the Waldorf school I was afraid of not having the moral support of teachers, friends and family I'd always known. After a couple weeks in Aspen High School, I saw that although the teachers weren't like Waldorf teachers, they were there for you, too. It was the same with friends. I wanted to keep my Waldorf friends but also start anew. I adapted easily. Basketball has always been my first love, but I played soccer and competed in track and field in high school too. For the past four summers I've volunteered with the Aspen Youth Experience, an organization that brings inner-city kids here to show them another world that's beautiful and fun, where they're respected and trusted.

Brittany rock climbing

I've been playing recreation basketball since first grade. I'm now a senior and team captain. This summer, I played on a competitive Denver team that traveled all around the country and so began getting inquiries from colleges. What I want to study changes daily, but probably a subject related to environmental studies. I loved history in the Waldorf school, which we studied in great depth. We then used our imaginations creating a main lesson book from cover-to-cover. I wouldn't have had the chance to express myself doing art every day in a public school. My little cousin is starting school this year and we've talked my aunt into sending her to a Waldorf school, too.

Last year my basketball coach was on a teacher exchange in Ireland and when he returned, I was talking to him about his experience. I got the idea of touring there with our team. We started planning it that day, raised the money and this June, the whole team toured Ulster, Belfast, Dublin, Limerick and other cities playing basketball. I know Waldorf kids aren't known for being "street smart," but I found I was the one getting my teammates out of the bus and into the towns to see the historical places and appreciate the art. I think interest in the world is one of the gifts of Waldorf education.

Alexandra Fortier and Brittany Fortier

Tae Westcott

Tae joined Patty Fox's class as the only boy and the only third grader when the class was officially in the fourth grade curriculum. He graduated from eighth grade with ten others who had joined the combined class over the years.

After being with people I'd known for years, I worried about making friends in high school, but it was a non-issue. I made great friends through soccer and Nordic skiing and my main interest, having fun! Working with textbooks and taking tests was more of a problem, but I liked it all.

I'm studying exercise science now at Fort Lewis College and thinking of coaching or becoming a physical education teacher or personal trainer but I'm not ready to commit. I'm taking the winter semester off to train in free skiing, aiming toward the X-Games, although I expect only to compete in the trials this year.

Sometimes I think I might have been a better test-taker if I hadn't gone to the Waldorf school – but I would have missed the pentathlon in fifth grade and all of our great class trips, especially the trip to the Oregon Shakespeare Festival. That was the best.

Tamas Bates-Solomon

Tamas started second grade with Patty Doyle, created chaos with Robin Marcus, joined Patty Fox's class for third through eight grade, then returned to his original class to graduate! Where did it lead? His mother, Bates, wrote to the school:

Upon Tamas Bates-Solomon's high school graduation

Tamas, still on the planet

I know how important it is for you, as a young school, to know what has become of your early graduates. But also I know how each and every one of you wrung your hands and suffered over this particular student, and I wanted you, as individuals and teachers, to know how profound and beneficial your efforts have been in shaping a young person's life. And thank you, truly every one who had a hand in "keeping Tamas on the Planet" as Doug Sheffer used to say, so that he could become the adult person that he is today.

Tamas has done very well since graduating from the Waldorf School on the Roaring Fork. He has had an amazingly calm and productive adolescence and as a young man, he is quiet and thoughtful with a great deal of understanding and patience for others. He can do math and spell without using paper and is taking piano lessons. I add this because his music and evaluations at the school were… well, a different story. All of this results from the school except that I think if he could sleep inside of his computer, he would. He listened to everything that anybody at the Waldorf school ever said, and he has steadily worked away at it ever since because he always felt that everyone there at the school believed in him. Tamas is likely to major in computer science, but he says if he ever has a second choice he will become a Waldorf teacher. And he always urges everyone he meets who is interested in teaching to pursue eurythmy.

Brittany Fortier, Tamas and new friend

Tamas graduated in June, 2005, from Bellevue High School, Washington with honors. He also received his AA degree in August from Bellevue Community College. His very impressive high school portfolio is on file in the office.

Kelsea Mulcahy, pictured with her horse, Lightning, is a champion barrel racer

Glenn Engelman

Glenn learned "form" in the Waldorf school – and applies it in every aerial maneuver.

I was in the first kindergarten in the Waldorf school and went through fifth grade with Patty Doyle and Robin Marcus, but when the school moved downvalley, I wanted to stay in Aspen. I had started playing soccer and basketball, had met a group of kids I liked and felt I needed a bigger group. I thought I'd taken what I could from Waldorf and when Robin left, I decided to give the public school a try. I knew I'd keep in touch with Matt Fox and Tristan Kanipe no matter what, and I have.

The change was very hard at the time but in the long run, was good for me. Of course, there were many things I learned at the Waldorf school that I wouldn't have learned in the public school, especially all of the handwork, creative skills and how to learn in a healthier and happier environment. I also learned drama and eurythmy and singing and I appreciate the work that goes into performance. This has made me more open-minded about a lot of things than some of my public school classmates. I was experiencing the world in creative, imaginative ways while they were taking standardized tests in third grade, so I see things from a whole different mind-set.

Outside the classroom, my main interests have been freestyle skiing and tennis. As a senior, I'm the captain of both teams and have also been coaching tennis and teaching clinics and private lessons for the past few summers. In college, I'm thinking of studying psychology and sports medicine, perhaps sports psychology, but I also plan to compete in skiing on the professional level. I'm taking mostly International Baccalaureate classes, and will be able to choose from several colleges where I can also compete in skiing.

AVSC skier makes history at nationals

■ Engelman hangs with top U.S. guns in dual moguls

Contributed report

Glenn Engelman saved his best for last once again at the U.S. National Championships in Park City, Utah, last weekend, March 24-26.

The 17-year-old Aspen Valley Ski and Snowboard Club (AVSC) moguls specialist went toe to toe with top U.S. freestylers, including most of the World Championship U.S. Freestyle Team, and had some surprising results in Saturday's dual moguls competition.

Engelman qualified for nationals as the top discretionary pick for the Rocky Mountain Division based on his total points for the season. He and the rest of the AVSC qualifiers, including Rachel Weitzenkorn, Kaitlin Mickes and Sam Ferguson, had the advantage... Park City competiti...

Engelman, AVSC up to challenge on home turf

Aspen Times staff report

The AVSC freestyle team was up to the challenge on its home turf as the Aspen Valley Ski and Snowboard Club played host to the top freestyle skiers in a Rocky Mountain ...moguls slopestyle...

Jimmy Disco, for the win.

"He had the lead and was winning when he lost a ski in the middle of the course," said Knight. "He was skiing so well I didn't even realize he had lost it until about two turns later when he pulled off to the side."

Engelman finished with second place ...sition and the event is sure...

Freestyle moguls skier Glenn Engelman at the U.S. National Championships last weekend in Park City, Utah. Courtesy photo/AVSC.

AVSC freestyle team member Glenn Engelman pulls an iron cross during last weekend's moguls competition at Aspen Highlands. Photo courtesy Steve Hach.

Matt Fox

Matt was the oldest child in the first kindergarten and when there was no class for him, he started first grade in the public school. Miserable and missing his friends, he joined his mother's third grade at Christmas and Patty Doyle's combined class the next year, a class that grew to include six other students his age.

When I graduated from the Waldorf school in 2001, I was the only person going to Aspen High School so I was concerned about friendships. I knew kids I'd played sports with my whole life though, and I liked all the kids on the Aspen Valley Ski Club team. They became my best friends as we traveled around the state to competitions that sometimes took us out of school for a week at a time. Ski racing made it difficult to keep up with my International Baccalaureate classes, but at graduation I was named Scholar Athlete and awarded two environmental scholarships which were real honors. It was equally rewarding to serve as team captain for both skiing and baseball and to win the state championships in skiing my senior year.

I was concerned with reading when I started high school because I've always been a slow reader, but I found I just had to allow more time than others to complete assignments. Test-taking didn't present a problem either. I enjoyed writing and math in high school but my favorite subject was IB Physics. I'm now considering mechanical engineering at Colorado State University because engineers are finding so many cool ways to help the environment.

It's hard for me to know how I'm different from other people because of my Waldorf experience. I only know what I've lived. People comment on how athletic Waldorf students are and have attributed that to eurythmy. I just know I'm glad to have made the CSU baseball team as a lefty pitcher. I'm sure my concern for the environment comes both from Waldorf education and from having spent summers backpacking with my family. In the future, I'll be able to see the influence Waldorf had on me more clearly.

Tristan Kanipe

Matt, Glenn and Tristan "hung out" together in kindergarten – and are still best friends.

I entered Aspen High School in 2002 concerned with my ability to take tests and make friends in a school that was five times larger than the Waldorf school. Friendships are often formed in elementary and middle school and I was afraid I wouldn't find a social niche. My experience turned out surprisingly well. The kids were great and very accepting. I was much better at test-taking than I thought I would be, better than many of my public school classmates. In fact, I've had all A's except for one B-plus in high school.

My main extracurricular interest has been theater, with a second interest in baseball. I like theater and have been told I'm good at it. The acting is fun because you get to step into another personality for an hour or two. I was the paper boy in the Aspen Theatre in the Park production of *Picnic* when I was a

Tristan Kanipe, Matt Fox and Glenn Engelman

freshman, and Rolf in the Aspen Community Theatre production of *The Sound of Music* as a junior. I've now become more involved in the technical aspects of theater and have worked as the light board operator and master electrician this summer for Theatre Aspen. Loren Wilder, a professional in lighting design, has taken me under her wing. I like being hands-on, knowing how things work and how to fix things that don't. This winter I'll be lighting corporate events for her local company, Seymour Productions.

Theater, of course, was part of the Waldorf curriculum and I was well prepared for high school theater. Another attribute from Waldorf was memorization, which is all that's required for passing tests in high school. But the greatest contribution of my Waldorf education was the ability to learn. I can sit down and figure out any assignment, then apply it to new situations and expand it into other fields of study. I want to earn an MBA in college because I think that no matter what I find that I love, I'll be able to turn it into a successful business.

Brooke Sheffer

Brooke was another "founding" kindergartener.

Brooke with her self-portrait painted in high school

When I transferred to Aspen High School, I was not too worried about the adjustment period. I was fortunate enough to fly through the academic requirements even though I was taking some of the most challenging classes available; however, I lacked "street smarts." I had a genuine trust for everyone around me and the thought of academic dishonesty did not even cross my mind. I learned how naïve I was when a classmate I thought I was collaborating with used my work and called it her own. I was terrified that there was going to be hazing; luckily, there was no real threat, simply a large age gap. I had no idea how much personal growth takes place during high school, and truly believed that the four-year age difference between 14 and 18 was insignificant. This, however, was not the case, and I quickly discovered that, upon entering high school, there is much to learn.

My main interests in high school have been in the visual and performing arts. I will have taken ten classes in visual arts when I graduate. I was a nun in the Aspen Community Theatre production of *The Sound of Music*, I played one of the four troublemaker girls in the high school production of *The Boyfriend*, and have worked backstage in other productions. I have also been involved in our literary magazine, Nepsa Merge, and the prom committee. Outside of school, I've been showing my horse in hunter/jumper shows around the state. I have attended a class on Genomics and DNA through the Aspen Science Center, and have participated in several Aspen Institute seminars: Teen Socrates, Great Ideas, and the Aspen Ideas Festival 2005.

I am ecstatic to begin the next chapter of my life. I am currently looking into college out of state or possibly out of the country. I intend to visit Oxford and Cambridge in England, and St. Andrews in Scotland. I am unsure whether or not I want to major in psychology, but am certain that I want to minor in visual or performing arts. Because of the Waldorf school and its curriculum, art has always been a huge part of my life, and it will most definitely be crucial to my future. Beyond art, the greatest benefit that Waldorf afforded me is deep self-love. The personal support that I received from the beginning of my schooling has given me enormous awareness of the value of individuality. Having such caring people encourage me from an early age made me see how important it is to discover who I really want to be, and let that person shine. To me, Waldorf is an excellent alternative school that strives to motivate students by guiding them down the path to self-discovery and exploration through carefully monitored growth.

Dustin Braeger

I graduated from the Waldorf School on the Roaring Fork in 2001 with seven years of Waldorf experience under my belt. From this point, I took on the academics of Glenwood Springs High School and ended up doing rather well, playing three sports all four years and graduating first in my class, valedictorian.

To give you a little background on my family, I grew up in a single-parent home where my mother, who is a kindergarten teacher at the Waldorf school, has done an amazing job at raising both my sister and me on her own. Since my high school graduation in 2005, I have gone on to Pepperdine University, Seaver College, where I am currently majoring in sports medicine. My dream for the future is to one day go to medical school and become an orthopedic surgeon.

Grace Schultz

As my Aspen High School teachers say, I am highly motivated, not for the grades but for the education. I think the excellent International Baccalaureate staff really appreciates that about me, and I appreciate them. Academically, the transition to high school has been an easy one and I think most Waldorf students are surprised about how far ahead they are in math and history.

I've had three main interests in high school. First, I've been involved in fifteen theater productions in high school, from starring roles to chorus to backstage. I will continue with this passion in the future. My second interest is international relations. Although it's taken three years of hard work, I've started a Model United Nations club at our school and this spring we're going to Costa Rica to participate in our first competition. My third interest is psychology and I'm thinking about ways to tie all of these interests together in college. I've participated in a number of other organizations, too. The Aspen Youth Council, which advises the Aspen City Council on youth issues,

the earth club, the drama club, Heroes and the kayak club.

I'm hoping to attend a small, liberal arts college because I value the student-teacher relationships that I've known in the Waldorf school and the high school. Hampshire College and Amherst are at the top of my list right now. I also plan to study abroad, possibly at Oxford because of their theater department.

I am very thankful and proud of my Waldorf education and would not trade it for the world! Through Waldorf I was able to grow as an individual and gain an incredible education at the same time. It was through Waldorf that my passions were inspired and some of my closest friendships were formed.

Isabelle DeLise

Isabelle was the youngest "founder" in the Aspen Waldorf School.

Isabelle rock climbing near Independence Pass

I graduated from the Waldorf School on the Roaring Fork after twelve wonderful years of schooling. For eight of the twelve I was taught by the same class teacher, Frances Lewis. I learned in detail the fascinating history of Greek art, sailed the Mediterranean with Odysseus, learned of Hannibal and his elephants, Roman battles and the first American presidents.

I studied the Renaissance and the Depression, world revolutions and revolutions in science. I was taught to sing, dance, speak with poise, recite poems, and perform a Shakespearean play. In those years, I was taught to play the violin, cello, recorder and flute. I am 17 years old and I can still remember a fourteen-line sonnet from eighth grade.

I now attend Aspen High School. My favorite subjects are English, history and art. I struggle a bit with left-brain activities like math and science but I very much enjoy giving oral presentations in front of a full class, or being tucked deep into an oil painting, aware only of the stroke of my paint brush. I like to read and listen to music, rock climb and swim in ice cold rivers. I appreciate the outdoors. All those things my Waldorf education taught me to love.

I must admit my first sight of the new public school made me a bit nervous. Would I be able to take tests? Could I pass math? Would I fit in? I chuckle at those worries now. School has been a piece of cake for me – with maybe a few bites out of it. It was not a problem for me to transfer and I couldn't have been better prepared for high school. I am interested in environmental studies at the moment and may look into Evergreen College a year from now. I could also see myself in a people-related field, doing presentations, teaching or maybe working in outdoor leadership. Whatever the future may hold, my past schooling will always influence it. I thank my mentors for preparing me for a challenging world. I feel well-rounded and ready for new influences.

Claire Westcott

Claire joined Frances Lewis' first grade in 1994.

Going from the Waldorf school to Aspen High School where I am now a junior has been very easy for me. I was well prepared and have been investigating all sorts of classes. In the Waldorf school I loved art, drama and history, which are the three areas I'm still most interested in. Although I don't know where I'll go to college, I know I want to do something with acting. I loved being in class plays at the Waldorf school, and in high school I have continued to be thrilled with acting. I also remember taking so much time drawing pictures in my main lesson book and going "above and beyond" with my paintings. I think the Waldorf school helped bring out these strengths and open my eyes to all the wonders of the world.

Stella Doble

Stella came to kindergarten in 1992, the second year of the school.

After having gone to the Waldorf school for ten years, I was fully ready for my next big adventure, Aspen High School. Any 13-year-old is nervous about going into high school, and having attended a private school all my life, I was too. But I was not afraid of not being liked. Rather, high school was full of things I had seldom used: computers, textbooks and power point presentations. The work I was preparing to do, and do now, is very different from the work I did at Waldorf. My teachers no longer require that I hand-write my papers; in fact, they prefer them typed. Drawing a beautiful picture and perfecting my cursive is no longer important, even though using these skills still help me rake in the extra-credit points on my projects. After the initial shock of high school wore off, I found I wasn't behind everyone else and was even ahead in history and art. My only real disadvantage was my lack of computer skills. With my slow typing and poor knowledge of computers, my papers took a little longer than I would have liked. I soon caught on and now, in my junior year, I'm just as proficient as the next person.

Being a Waldorf student didn't just put me ahead academically, it also influenced my personality and my outlook on education. It seems to me that many kids were already burned out on school and learning when they got into high school, but I was ready to extend my horizons, and because of my unique education, I have that same curiosity today. Although I'm not sure which college I will attend, I plan to major in a subject that will assure me of a job helping others and hopefully making a difference in their lives.

My time spent at the Waldorf School on the Roaring Fork was filled with learning of a very different kind than that at Aspen High School. There are many paths through education, some more trodden than others, and I'm wholeheartedly glad that my parents took the one less traveled.

Isabelle DeLise, Claire Westcott and Stella Doble

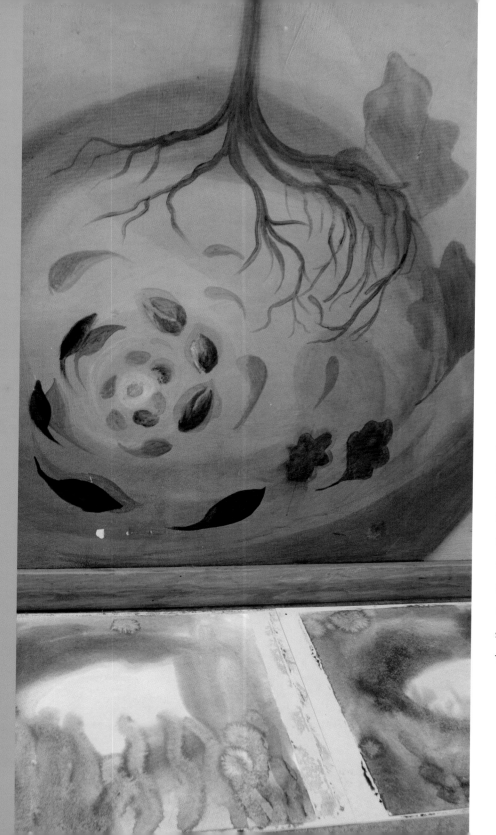

Who was Rudolf Steiner?

Adapted in part from "Rudolf Steiner, A sketch of his life and work," by John Davy in Waldorf Education, A Family Guide, edited by Pamela Johnson Fenner and Karen L. Rivers

"Trying to write something about Rudolf Steiner and the educational impulse he generated is like trying to say something about life. Where do you begin? Where do you stop? What do you include? What do you leave out?" These words open M.C. Richards' description of the Waldorf initiative, *Toward Wholeness: Rudolf Steiner Education in America*. Indeed, it is very hard to narrow Steiner's extraordinary life and works to a brief description. In more than 6,000 lectures and 150 books, Steiner sought to explain his insights into education, medicine, agriculture, architecture, economics and human rights, religious practices, movement – that is, the human condition – and his students are still trying to fully grasp the implications of his work.

Steiner was born in 1861 in a peasant village in Lower Austria, the gifted son of a railway official. His father, a freethinker, encouraged him to seek a scientific education rather than join the clergy, as most poor but talented young men did. Supporting himself through tutoring, Steiner took degrees in mathematics, physics and chemistry and was befriended by a famous Goethe scholar, Karl Julius Schroer, at whose invitation he began to edit Goethe's scientific works. He moved to Weimar where he remained for seven years, meeting and exchanging ideas with leading figures of Central European culture while struggling internally with the spiritual insights he had known since childhood. In 1894, he published *The Philosophy of Freedom*, a sober and direct examination of his spiritual research.

Disappointed in the book's reception, Steiner moved to Berlin to edit an avant-garde literary magazine. Although he associated with poets and playwrights seeking alternative social and political forms, he refused to support any party line. When he published an essay titled "Goethe's Secret Revelations," a discussion of *The Green Snake and the Beautiful Lily*, his radical, materialistic-scientific circle was shocked. Only the spiritually-oriented members of the Theosophical Society embraced his ideas.

Steiner perceived that humanity stood ready to understand the relationship between earthly and spiritual life in a new way. Creative impulses able to transform modern culture stood ready, but human beings had to undergo rigorous self-development in order to access these fresh forces.

Steiner's realization prompted him to speak directly of his spiritual research. "[My] heartfelt desire [was] to introduce into life the impulses from the world of the spirit…but for this, there was no understanding." Nonetheless, within a short period, "Steiner surveyed with clarity and intimacy the spiritual realities at work in the kingdoms of nature and the cosmos, the inner nature of the human soul and spirit and their potential for further development, the nature and practice of meditation, the experiences of the soul before birth and after death, the spiritual history and evolution of humanity and the earth, and detailed studies of the workings of reincarnation and karma." (Davy p 15).

Steiner began to lecture widely on his spiritual research, often giving more than one lecture a day. In 1913, the foundation stone for a center for anthroposophic study was laid in Dornach, Switzerland. This extraordinary building, formed in wood and built by international volunteers when their nations were at war, was nearing completion on December 31, 1922, when it was burned to the ground by an arsonist. On the next morning, Steiner laid the foundation for the Anthroposophical Society which continues Steiner's research into "the wisdom of the human being" today. The second Goetheanum, completed after Steiner's death, serves as a center for the society and a world-renowned venue for performances of eurythmy, Steiner's Mystery Plays, Goethe's *Faust* and many other plays and concerts.

Anthroposophy

First described by Rudolf Steiner (1861-1925), Anthroposophy, or "wisdom of the human being" concerns itself with the interaction of the human being and the spiritual world. In this worldview, the human being is seen as a microcosm of the universe; an individual who attains true self-knowledge thereby comes to understand the world. Conversely, a striving to comprehend the world and humanity is also a path to self-knowledge. With its rigorous epistemological foundations and its focus on spiritual enlightenment as a path of knowledge, Anthroposophy, a path for adults, also serves as a solid foundation for the unfolding of the child through Waldorf education.

At the close of World War I, Emil Molt, owner of the Waldorf Astoria Cigarette Factory in Stuttgart, Germany, asked Steiner to speak to his disheartened factory workers. The workers had been shocked by the horrors of destruction they had witnessed and depressed by the apparently fruitless daily tasks they performed. Steiner's lectures on economics, trade and the "threefold social order," which he envisioned as a new possibility for social structure, so encouraged the workers that they asked that a school be opened in which their children would be taught in this way. Steiner was waiting for such a request and moved quickly to gather experts from many walks of life who supported his work to become the first Waldorf teachers. His lectures to them form the body of Waldorf and curative education.

"Steiner's social thinking can only be adequately grasped in the context of his view of history, which he saw as shaped fundamentally by inner changes in human consciousness in which higher spiritual beings are actively participating... [We] cannot expect to build a healthy social order except on the basis of a true and deep insight not only into the material but also into the soul and spiritual nature and needs of human beings as they are today." (Davy p 16).

Steiner died on March 30, 1925, having planted seeds of renewal in virtually every field of human endeavor. Biodynamic agriculture, anthroposophically-extended medicine, the new arts of eurythmy and speech-formation, and, of course, Waldorf education, are just a few of the myriad impulses he pioneered.

The Waldorf School on the Roaring Fork owes its existence to Rudolf Steiner's comprehensive philosophy, and owes its sustenance to the many people who have found a connection to his profound educational methodology. Over the fourteen years described in this book, teachers, parents, staff, and friends have united their own path of development with the school's growth and unfolding. We hope and trust that our school will continue to serve as a bridge between what Rudolf Steiner termed "the world of the senses and the world of the spirit." We are resolved to be a setting in which our children will develop into adults who work in the world with wakefulness, responsibility, and love.

The Stars spoke once to Man.
It is World-destiny
That they are silent now.
To be aware of the silence
Can become pain for earthly Man.
But in the deepening silence
There grows and ripens
What Man speaks to the Stars,
To be aware of the speaking
Can become strength for Spirit-Man
Rudolf Steiner

Afterword

As any parent who has received a school report on his or her fourteen-year-old knows, by the time the words were put to paper, their youngster had already changed, sometimes beyond recognition! Growth and development make for ceaseless change – in the life of a growing school no less than in the life of a growing child – and the Waldorf School on the Roaring Fork is no exception. With this in mind, as we make our book ready for publication, we would like to catch you up with the present-day, sixteen-year-old Waldorf School on the Roaring Fork as it enters the 2006-2007 school year.

As we approach the autumn of 2006, our enrollment has grown to 175 students. We are fast approaching our current capacity of 200. Our graduates continue to stand out in the local community and our "Alumni Nights" are an inspiration for new parents as well as for faculty.

In our formative years, like a youngster ceaselessly outgrowing her clothes, our rapid development time and again challenged the organizational forms that we created. As we approach our mid-teens, we have become better prepared to meet our present and future needs. Our school structure has continued to grow stronger with the three governing bodies, the community council, the pedagogical council and the board working together. All the bodies work with consensus, each body governing in its realm of expertise, while the other bodies give feedback and input where appropriate.

All the bodies work with consensus, with each council governing in its realm of expertise and receiving feedback and input where appropriate from the other councils. The community council, along with the administrative coordinator, continues to work to support the teachers and the pedagogical council. Its members oversee the governance of the school, involving themselves in matters as diverse as the maintenance of the bus and the day-to-day implementation of the budget to issues involving personnel.

The mentoring support team previously mentioned has gained new members and has now become the pedagogical council. This body oversees the work of the teachers and students in the classroom, concerning itself with parent questions, curriculum, and the mentoring and evaluation of teachers. Our full-time faculty coordinator works in support of this body, organizing many of the details and serving as a channel for parent concerns. In many Waldorf schools a council with these tasks is formally founded as a "College of Teachers," and is thus officially entrusted with responsibility for the pedagogical and spiritual life of the school as well as the management of personnel. We hope to formally found this college this autumn, even as this book is being published. This is a very big step for a Waldorf school to take, and we know that our readiness to form this body is another sign that we are at a new stage in our development.

The board of trustees has recently gained new members and is strengthening the fundraising in the school. This past year (2005 – 2006) we far exceeded our goal for the Annual Giving campaign. We hope to begin a capital campaign in the near future to complete the building of our campus and to add to the already generous endowment we have received.

In addition, our parent council continues to support the parents of the community with a strong involvement in the festival life of the school, setting a fine example for the parent body and for the children. It also administers a good shepherd program for families in need and a buddy system for incoming families.

Two signs of a maturing school are a growing proportion of trained teachers and the faculty retention. We are pleased to report that eleven of our fourteen full-time teachers are fully trained as Waldorf teachers, and the other three are completing their Waldorf training. Three of these fourteen are full-time specialty teachers in movement, handwork, and eurythmy. In addition, we have a fully trained and experienced Waldorf remedial specialist assisting our teachers with assessments of children and working with students. We have only two new full-time faculty members joining us this year, one as our first grade teacher and the other replacing a teacher who will now be full-time in her specialty. Teachers are staying with the school, and our eighth grade teacher from last year is even returning to teach woodworking. We all agree that we love working with this faculty and feel privileged to work in this school we all hold so dear.

Like a garden filled with an abundance of beauty and nourishment, the Waldorf curriculum needs constant attention and intensive labor to remain vital. The faculty works tirelessly to bring the ideals of this remarkable curriculum into the life of the classroom.

After long study and collegial discussion we have adopted curriculum standards that we feel are appropriate for a Waldorf school in both math and language arts and we are working to strengthen the middle school curriculum in these areas. We are so confident in the rigorous standards that we have set that we are about to begin the process of accreditation, both with the Colorado Association of Independent Schools and with the Association of Waldorf Schools in North America. This dual accreditation will mark the crossing of an important threshold; when it is granted, the Waldorf School on the Roaring Fork will begin its progression into "young adulthood," a stage of new maturity and growing responsibility.

Although the parents, teachers, staff, and friends whose voices are heard in this book hold many points of view, we know that they would all agree that the Waldorf School on the Roaring Fork was, is, and will remain a work in progress and no less importantly, a work in process. Johann von Goethe, whose words helped inspire the cultural impulses that live in the Roaring Fork Valley, once said, "We honor the girl for what she is and the boy for what he will become." We hope that this book has revealed and celebrated our school from both of these perspectives.

The Making of...

RAISING
Waldorf

**The Building
of the
Waldorf School
on the
Roaring Fork**

*The Bookies: Front: Lynn Crawford, Doug Sheffer, Stevan Maxwell. Middle: Eleanor Jacobs, Stewart Oksenhorn. Back: J.Sue Robertson, Patty Fox.
Not pictured: Eugene Schwartz and Barbi Sheffer.*

We planted Steven Moore's ashes under a plum tree in the school yard in July of 2004. At this time of remembrance, Doug approached Patty with his wish to sponsor a written and photographic history of the Waldorf School on the Roaring Fork. He envisioned a beautiful coffee table book that would inform and inspire its readers. Once Patty was on board the team quickly assembled. Eleanor, a veteran organizer of many AWS and WSRF events, suggested asking Stevan and Lynn, who had produced a beautiful brochure for the school the year before to work on the project. Stewart, an Aspen Children's Garden parent and arts editor of The Aspen Times, agreed to work with Patty as her editor. Patty began the interview and writing process and Stewart reviewed the narrative as it developed. Eleanor scheduled and assisted during the photo shoots. Steve began photographing the people and the school. Lynn poured over historical photos gathered by Eleanor and a conception of the book's format emerged. At the end of the first year, an exemplary draft of the book existed. The engaging stories, beautiful photographs and professional layout were cause for celebration. J.Sue joined our group to shepherd the book through the next stages of editing and publication. Eugene Schwartz and Barbi Sheffer were invaluable resources and worked tirelessly proofing drafts for accuracy.

Now, we have brought our two-year endeavor to you hoping that you will embrace what we offer, forgive us any oversights or errors and profit from our experiences.

Index